The
ENEMY
INSIDE

Reflections of "ME"

BILL BALBACH

www.xulonpress.com

TABLE OF CONTENTS

ACKNOWLEDGEMENTS

Shelly and the boys- for always being a tremendous source of encouragement. I love following Jesus with you!

The Leadership at Impact Christian Church- for your patience and example. Your dedication to Jesus is contagious and it is an absolute joy to serve alongside you.

Xulon Press- for all your hard work in making this book a reality. I appreciate the opportunity.

Edit 24-7.com- your honesty and professionalism were a tremendous help in this process.

Amy- for your support and wisdom.

Doug- for your friendship and encouragement.

My in-laws- for accepting me into your family as one of your own.

My parents- for being an example in my life.

INTRODUCTION

P ayday hits. Bills get paid in a methodical order based on due dates and money available. Life stressors increase as an awareness settles in that living is expensive. Physical, emotional, and financial heartache creep up to an overwhelming level that blocks us from the "fullness of life" that Jesus promised.

The aftermath of this whirlwind from life drives us down a detour, which seems to bypass all the joy we once had, leaving us to realize that not only is life expensive, but the sum of our journey has delivered the conclusion that we are not really living. Existence has become our purpose.

Maybe one day, life will be more than the mere attempt to exist. Maybe one day our dreams will come true. Maybe one day we will realize the joy that Jesus gives through a lifestyle of significance and purpose. Maybe one day we will realize who we are.

Maybe that *one day* could be today. It seems that so often our lives have become like kindling, which ignites the fire so that it burns bright and fierce. Sadly, this spark of passion in life only lasts a moment. Without more fuel, the fire quickly fades.

There was a time in our lives when passion ignited—when our hearts were fully engaged with purpose and direction—until a fog set into the soul that revealed misery and confusion. How do we define ourselves? Where will our lives end up? Is there purpose? Is there significance?

To rekindle that passion into a fire that can sustain, there needs to be something more. In James 1, we learn that joy is found in the midst of heartache. Through trial, we find a stronger faith that develops perseverance. Perseverance guides us to a satisfied life.

Struggles with our ability to persevere and to identify purpose in our lives tend to be created

when our relationship with Jesus is disconnected. Faith has progressed into a journey of
weekly rituals, rather than a daily relationship.
An identity crisis within our faith has masked
our ability to recognize who we are in Christ.

Jesus died on the cross to give us a life of purpose for all eternity. Following Jesus demands
responsibility. It is the realization of the heart
of God activated in our lives.

Taking an aerial shot of David's life, we get
a glimpse into the difficulties he faced as his
journey paralleled that of King Saul. Becoming
a man after God's own heart, as the Bible
describes him, David found himself in a constant battle within his own heart, overcoming
the enemy inside to find himself standing strong.

Facing the recurring internal spiritual bat-
tles, we are often left discouraged by what
appears to be a lack of forward motion in our
faith. Attempting to persuade us away from
Jesus, the devil desires to bring chaos into our
souls. Enticing us towards poor choices, Satan
appears at times to have a stranglehold on
our hearts.

Still, there is hope in the end. While journeying with David, we will encounter his hardships and the mistakes he made in order to discover the path he took to overcome. See 1 & 2 Samuel for the full story of David and Saul.

Following Jesus can be challenging at times. The journey is long because the enemy is fierce, yet the battle is already won. Those that finish the race by standing firm in their faith will win. That hope is secure. Getting from here to there is what can be overwhelming.

Like David, you will fall. At times, you will mess up, but it is not about how you start—it is about how you finish.

Chapter 1

"ME" DEFINED

———————◦◦———————

"**M**irror, mirror on the wall..."[1] is a classic fairytale line leaving children of many different generations pondering their existences. Gazing into a personal, magical mirror is a struggle within the heart and a fierce battle with self-identity. This battle reveals that one's own magical mirror can be rather harsh, piercing through external appearances into the reality of the heart's condition: a desperate desire to be accepted and revered.

Looking into the mirror provides us an ability to examine ourselves. The reflections we see can bring us immense joy or plunge our hearts into the pit of despair. Oftentimes, these reflections unmask the reality of our hearts and turn us away from real joy.

Everyone faces a similar battle. Whether we realize it or not, we have infestations taking grip of our hearts. Like ants slowly taking over a house, unforeseen trigger points like jealousy, pride, guilt, and even resentment overwhelm our hearts. These emotions maintain the ability to transform us into a person who we never thought existed. Being motivated by the pain and struggles that exist within often causes the way we interact with the world to reflect the enemy inside.

Many popular comic book characters are the results of experiments gone wrong. We read about what happens to normal people who, when overwhelmed with extreme emotional distress, transform into completely different beings. This transformation may sometimes be for the good. Many times, though, we see evil unmasked within characters from virtuous beginnings who find themselves overwhelmed with personal demons that they can neither control nor remove.

Too often, in our personal journeys through life, we find ourselves having a similar struggle, transformed by an inward demon that haunts our hearts and reveals itself through emotional scars. Inwardly battling jealousy, anger, guilt, sadness, and other emotional enemies that tightly grip our hearts, we often lose our ability to realize hope. We don't want the internal scars to overtake our lives, but our hearts are nonetheless overwhelmed and must struggle against the following transformation.

As our hearts becomes infested, we find ourselves focused on the mirror of our souls, wondering what have we become. Buried beneath the weight of this world, bullied by the welts of our pain, we seek to identify our true selves.

Facing this mirror, we are left with the questions: Who am I? What defines me?

Sometimes we have separated ourselves from reality, not even recognizing the fact that we are lost. Like a man unwilling to ask for directions, we travel down the interstate of life thinking we can arrive at the destination on our own. Thus our hearts simply drive in an emotional circle with no end in sight, continually hitting the same pitfalls. If uncontrolled, our internal struggles will eventually open the floodgates of heartache into every other relationship. Raising children can unmask this reality for us. Children often undeservedly lose their innocence because of the uncontrolled rampage that conflicts the heart of a parent. These pitfalls can be avoided only when the skirmishes of the heart are brought to light and dealt with.

In the New Testament, we are introduced to a man who wrestled with some of the same dilemmas. While we often acknowledge him with high honors, the apostle Paul was simply a man that strived to please God, but he faced struggles nonetheless.

Paul loved God and wanted to please him with his life more than anything. Even in the dark ages of his personal journey, when he was persecuting and killing Christians, Paul was trying to please God. Entrenched in the laws and customs of the Old Testament, Paul believed that this new Jesus movement disgraced the name of God and threatened to sway the people of Israel away from a good standing with God. While this was his initial motivation, the pride in Paul's heart blinded him from the ways in which God was working. His good intentions were lost due to the battle within.

Eventually, his soul was awakened while he traveled the road to Damascus to pursue more followers of Jesus (Acts 9). On this road he encountered Jesus, who was the focus of his attacks. Physically, Paul's eyes were blinded, but his heart was spiritually opened to the realization that Jesus is God. In that moment, reality crashed into the depths of his heart to demolish the emotional cycle that is commonly known as life. An encounter with the One who is the source of life brings hope, which can crush the weight of any burdens.

Life tends to cause an eclipse of our hearts from the realms of reality. It casts our notions of truth into shadowy disfiguration when our experiences override the reality of who God is. The Creator of all has a tremendous passion for humankind, who is the focus of His creation.

When our experiences blind us from the true workings of God, the enemy inside wins.

Our faith becomes a train wreck because our hearts are right, but our actions are off base. We love Jesus, but how we conduct our daily lives derails our faith. This battle of the heart was something that Paul continued to face, even years later when he was in God's good graces.

"I don't really understand myself," Paul says, describing his struggles, "for I want to do what is right, but I don't do it. Instead, I do what I hate" (Romans 7:15). Every person struggles with a similar identity crisis. We look in the mirror one day, amazed at the person we have become. In our younger years, we claimed that we would never go down a path like this. We find ourselves investigating our personal circumstances to identify how we became what we now see.

We desire to do good deeds, yet evil tends to wreak terror in our hearts, which leads to bitterness. Bitterness leads to blame, which causes minor issues to transform into broken relationships with family, friends, the church, and even with God. The blame game makes us put up

"ME" Defined

walls against those who matter most, causing more and more turmoil in our lives. This is how Satan desires to destroy us from the inside out. Questions like "how have I lost control?" consume the focus of our thoughts, moving us to the brink of emotional insanity.

To best answer those questions, let us get to the heart of Paul's thoughts in his letter to the Romans.

A better translation of Paul's meaning in Romans 7:15, would exchange the word "understand" with "to approve." In his commentary, Jack Cottrell identifies Paul's meaning as such: "An analogy would be one government's refusal to acknowledge or accept the validity of another government established by a coup or revolution in another country. The new government may be a fact, but it need not be acknowledged or recognized as legitimate. In this sense Paul says, 'Yes, I admit that sin sometimes takes control of me, but I do not acknowledge it as my true master; I do not accept the legitimacy of its rule over my life.'"[2]

19

In order to overcome the enemy that tends to dwell in our hearts, we need to step into reality on Paul's terms.

Who is your true master? Do you accept the rule of sin in your life?

Normalcy Of Your Life

In all honesty, what defines your life: the world or Jesus? Don't allow these questions to guilt you into being overly critical of yourself. The occasional goof-ups are not the point here. This is instead about reflecting on your existence to realize what patterns determine your everyday life.

In Paul's letter to the church in Galatia, he explains what it means to "walk in the Spirit" versus walking in the ways of the world, or indulging in acts of the flesh.

Take a moment to examine these two lists (from Galatians 5:19-23):

Acts of the flesh: sexual immorality, impurity, and excessive indulgences in sensual behaviors, idolatry and witchcraft, hatred, constantly creating disagreements, jealousy, fits of rage, selfish ambition, creating disunity, envy, drunkenness, orgies, and the like.

Fruits of the Spirit: love, joy, peace, patience, kindness, goodness, faithfulness, gentleness, and self-control.

With your lifestyle as an example, which list do you most relate to? Which list do you want to relate to? Who is your master: you, your desires, or your King? What defines your life?

To move forward, we must deal with these questions honestly. It is impossible to move ahead if we fail to recognize our current spiritual condition. We often find ourselves unable to take the next step in our faith simply because we are not being honest about our current spiritual states. Sometimes we are too hard on ourselves, keeping our faith stagnant. Other times we overestimate ourselves, trying to walk on water when we have not learned to swim. In either case, we neglect our abilities to grow spiritually.

Balancing our inner turmoil with our external actions is critical. Sometimes we live on spiritual life support because we continually act against God's desires. We find ourselves doing the very things that we challenge others to stop doing.

Remember, there is a difference between occasionally slipping and becoming a repeat offender. We acknowledge that we mess up, but like Paul said, we will not allow sin to become our masters: we will not allow it to rule our lives.

Unfortunately, too many times we find ourselves enjoying sin, which causes us to crave more of it. This hunger for sin moves us from the appetizer to the main course: over-indulgence, when a simple craving devolves into an unquenchable appetite for more. When sin becomes our master, wrongdoings transform into a dominant desire in our lives.

Desire may not be an accurate term for some to use. We may dislike those actions, but we cannot find a way to control them. Impatience, anger, and jealousy, among other things, are all possible causes.

Worldly acts distance us from God when they become more prominent in our lives, imprisoning

our hearts as they beat us down with unforeseen consequences.

Reality cannot be escaped. Every choice we
make and every action we commit has a consequence attached to it. Good or bad, we will face
some outcome from the directions we go. For
example, bitterness can destroy relationships,
while forgiveness can bring restoration. Society
has crumbled into a moral landslide because of
the misconception that we can do whatever we
want. "It is my life," we are encouraged to believe,
"and what I do does not affect anyone else. If it
does, it is someone else's problem, not mine."
This lie has transformed our understandings,
adjusted our actions, and has caused the world
to deteriorate.

Do you ever feel like you are part of a gener-
ational curse? Do unfortunate circumstances
with consequences that seem impossible to
avoid always seem to happen only to you? These
are trends that many fall prey to. The only way
to end these ongoing misfortunes is to finally
put an end to the consequences by choosing to

change the course of the family line and begin a new legacy.

Each of us has certain standards ingrained within us. These standards shape how we view the world and how we conduct our lives. Previous relationships, including friendships, familial relationships, work relationships, or romantic relationships, all affect our future relationships. We have been emotionally and spiritually shaped by the people of our past.

Our relationships and choices build the foundation of our lives. Sometimes there are cracks in our foundations from poor choices or broken relationships. The structure of our house is not secure because the strength of our foundations has been compromised by choices we have made or choices others have made concerning us. We tend to compound our fractured foundations with yet more poor choices. At some point the cycle needs to end. We must rise up and say, "NO MORE!"

More than likely, we are sharing our personal traits and the consequences of our choices with the people around us. It is not just our lives that are being affected.

To fix the cycle, the heart needs to be examined. Trigger points are like a ticking time bomb in our hearts. One moment, life is good. The next, our hearts get triggered by something someone says or does, and the inner enemy comes out.

"I have discovered this principle of life," Paul continues in Romans, "that when I want to do what is right, I inevitably do what is wrong. I love God's law with all my heart. But there is another power within me that is at war with my mind. This power makes me a slave to the sin that is still within me" (Romans 7:21-23).

Did you catch the slippery slope that Paul describes? Our hearts are in a constant battle of right against wrong, good choices against poor choices. Our sinful natures develop an unquenchable appetite for destruction. Although those desires may seem right and feel good for a time, they lead us down a dangerous path. We will inevitably slip and fall. We will make mistakes and mess up. If we are not careful, we will become slaves to sin, slaves to the consequences of our choices. What was once a desire turned into an indulgence. That indulgence became our master.

Identify The Source

To control this unwanted master, we must find and avoid its source. Too often, when we are overwhelmed by negative consequences, we find ourselves trying to fix the symptoms. The symptoms may be tempered, but more problems will arise.

My wife and I were blessed with three boys, the youngest of whom are twins. When our twins were newborns, they struggled with health issues. Constantly sick and unable to gain weight, they had to visit every specialist in the medical field. Nothing was working, and eventually the doctor diagnosed them with "failure to thrive." Feeling that we were at the end of the rope, we visited a nutritionist. After further testing, we learned that their bodies were not absorbing any nutrients. As a consequence, their diets underwent an extreme overhaul. They eventually began to gain weight, and their bodies matured. Today they are active and growing on a normal diet without any health issues.

Because we did not know the physical state the twins were in, we could not get them the proper help. Likewise, many of us need to realize the spiritual and emotional states that we are in. The warning signs have been activated. For too long, we have been running around trying to fix the symptoms instead of cutting off the source. For some of us, faith is holding on by threads. Our faith has stalled, and we have been spiritually diagnosed with "failure to thrive."

We must recognize the trigger points of the heart. Without honesty in this department, we will never be able to move forward. In the late 1980s, a commercial campaign was initiated to raise awareness of potential hardships. During the initiation of this campaign, newscaster Tom Brokaw explained that the more we are informed about an oncoming disaster, the more likely we are to do something about it.[3]

There is truth to this. If we understand the trigger points of our hearts and how those triggers will affect our lives, we will likely take appropriate action. We often live in denial, failing to realize or admit our hearts' reactions to the circumstances around us.

Trigger points come in all shapes and sizes. Our hearts tend to have reactions when other experiences trigger or remind us of those past episodes, including past relational hurts, abuse, or poor choices.

When the heart revisits those past experiences, it overwhelms us with thoughts and moves us to actions that can knock us off of God's course. At these low points of our lives, we find ourselves repeating Paul's words, "Oh, what a miserable person I am! Who will free me from this life that is dominated by sin and death?" (Romans 7:24). When the heart is triggered, it affects our entire lives.

In the Old Testament, we meet a young man named David, who was called by God for a purpose. In order to achieve that purpose, however, he had to overcome some difficult circumstances.

Before David came onto the scene, God's chosen prophets led Israel. The people were not

satisfied with these circumstances. They wan.
a king. They wanted to be like the other nations
that surrounded them. God heard their plea
and appointed Saul as the first king of Israel.
1 Samuel 9 reveals that Saul had the appearance of a king. He initially did well in this role.
Somewhere along the journey, though, his heart
changed. He changed from a man seeking God
into a man who acted as if God were getting in
his way.

We often travel on a similar road. We love
God. We want to please Him with our lives.
Somewhere along the way, however, our hearts
get in the way of God's heart. Our attitude shifts
from a desire to please God to a passion for our
own personal gains, an obsession with main-
taining the comforts of this world. Instead of
running toward God, we seem to being frustrated that God is getting in our way. We may
feel that we want to truly enjoy life, and He prevents us from achieving that. Some of us, like
the people of Israel, may feel that God is holding
out on us.

Either way, we find ourselves in Saul's position. The trigger points in our hearts have been activated. This entangles us in a matrix of internal conflict, allowing no escape from a perceived state of helplessness.

Attitude Adjustment

Our hearts have a tendency to circumvent God's will, slowly pushing away His wisdom as the influence in our lives. Attitude truly reveals the heart's condition. As the heart decays, a corrupted attitude is unmasked. Our attitude affects everything in our lives, including how we treat people, how we deal with certain circumstances, and the way we look at the future.

My twins were learning how to ride their bikes while we were on a family beach vacation. I had one goal on this vacation: we were not going home with training wheels. Each morning, before the crowds arrived, we went to the beach for a family bike ride. No training wheels were allowed. After continued failure, my boys' attitudes began to change. Excitement turned to frustration and a desire to quit became evident. They were done, but I knew they could do it. I knew they could ride simply because I saw them ride. They may have ridden for only five feet, but they did it.

In a fatherly moment that more resembled a football coach reprimanding his players, I got them on their bikes and told them to knock off the attitude. I believed in them and saw their abilities, but their attitudes were holding them back. Telling them to put their feet on the pedals, I gave them a push and they were off. Five feet turned into ten feet, to twenty feet, and then before I knew it they were riding on the beach. A simple attitude adjustment placed them on the pathway to success. Bad attitudes often cause us to miss our true potential. In those moments, God tends to force us into a sink-or-swim situation. We can rise to the occasion or to allow a disruptive attitude to hijack our potential.

Too often we have the ability to move forward with God, but our attitudes hold us back. Our attitudes keep us from experiencing life in the way that God desires.

Saul and David's Saga Begins

Through First Samuel, we see a decline in Saul's attitude. Chapter 13 reveals a person who becomes impatient with God and the prophet Samuel. Rather than waiting for Samuel to conduct the proper offerings to God, Saul chooses to do it himself.

Poor attitudes can send us down a path of independence from God and His bride, the church. We were never created to be alone. Like Saul, though, when our attitudes sour, we want to do things our own way rather than seek the heart of God. Instead of depending *on God*, we depend *on the self.* Seeking wisdom from *within,* as opposed to seeking wisdom from *above,* ultimately leads to poor choices.

After defeating the Philistines, Saul waited seven days for Samuel to arrive and conduct offerings to God. Saul grew tired of waiting and eventually decided to do the offerings himself. Samuel arrived as Saul was lighting the fire and trouble ensued.

Impatience engulfs the hearts of many. God does not arrive on "our schedule," nor does He answer prayers "our way." Our society's consumer mentality warps our attitudes, transforms our choices, and adjusts our paths. We have grown accustomed to a society defined by "wants."

We establish new ideas that we believe provide the freedom to live life our way, guilt-free. At least, that's what we think. We make choices to benefit personal agendas. Living the life of tranquility clouds our ability to see the danger that lies ahead. Making choices to please ourselves is extremely dangerous.

The end of this darkened road leads to unforeseen consequences that will alter any chosen destination. Saul's attitude led to poor choices. As a consequence, God tells him: "now your kingdom will not endure; the Lord has sought out a man after his own heart and appointed him ruler of his people, because you have not kept the Lord's command" (1 Samuel 13:14).

Saul eventually lost everything he had because he did not recognize or control the triggers of his heart. Every choice we make has an immediate consequence or a delayed consequence attached to it. Either way, the consequence is coming.

The choices we make are like a springboard that launches us either toward the heart and mission of God or further away from His plan. Saul's example is not one to be followed. The path is a destructive one.

Oftentimes, we are left inundated by the consequences of our own choices. Before we hit the panic button, let's discover the reality of God's grace. Grace is receiving that which we do not deserve. The fact that God is consistently on our sides, despite our shortcomings, is grace in action. Jesus coming to this world and dying on the cross is grace in action. God did not go through all of that to give up on us easily.

We do not lose God's grace, but we often miss out on His blessings because of the choices we make. By opposing His desires, we choose to walk away from the blessings that He wants to give.

God gave Saul chance after chance to do things the right way. But still, Saul chose his own way above God's way. Finally, God allowed him to walk his own path and receive his own consequences.

God told Saul another important detail: He was already preparing someone else to take his place. God made David the next king of Israel. David's preparation included years of agony, as he became prey to Saul's vicious attacks.

Throughout his journey, David was beaten down by life, and his daily circumstances became overwhelming. While life continually got harder, he lost support from the people he thought were on his side. David was different from Saul, however. Saul chased his own heart when things did not go his way. David, on the other hand, chased God.

Saul allowed sin to be his master. He did not control the pride that festered in his heart. Because he lacked trust, bitterness gripped Saul's heart and turned his hope into an internal rage over what he thought was lost control. Bitterness transformed his action, and he attempted to manipulate the workings of God into a self-centered journey.

David would not go that route. As Samuel was identifying David as the next king, God reminded him of a very important truth: "The Lord does not look at the things people look at. People look at the outward appearance, but the Lord looks at the heart" (1 Samuel 16:7b).

Looking at the mirror, what do you see? Venture into your soul; see your heart. See what God sees.

Life is not about getting knocked down. It is about getting back up. Now is the time to get back up, dust yourself off, and seek to define your life through Jesus instead of yourself. Find the life that he wants to give.

Personal Reflection

1. What do you see when you look in the mirror?

2. What struggles lurk in your heart?

3. Examine your life. Who is your master?

4. In what ways has your attitude affected your choices?

5. What steps can you take to refocus on God rather than on yourself?

Chapter 2

THAT DAY

———◦———

There are days that live in infamy and that we never forget. From personal moments to global catastrophes, our lives can change in an instant.

Certain situations can redirect us toward the abyss of the unknown. We fall asleep to a blissful evening when all seems well, only to wake and find the world turned upside down. Everyone will experience this, from a surprise pregnancy to the loss of a loved one. Some days give us no warnings beforehand and no explanations afterwards. The curveballs that life throws can be overwhelming—whether a tragic medical condition, a layoff, or some terrible consequence of choices we have made.

Sometimes, whether by our own doing or because of forces beyond our control, life disorients us with a new normal. In the Old Testament, we are introduced to a young man who faced a similar challenge. He would go on to shape the nation of Israel and carve the path for the coming Messiah.

David was selected as the next king of Israel. As the youngest of his family, he was the most unexpected choice. In fact, the day the prophet Samuel came to David's home probably sent a shockwave through his heart. I often wonder about David's heart during his journey to the throne of Israel. Life was not easy for him. He lived a quiet existence of tending his father's sheep until that day, when everything changed.

Not long after being anointed as the next king to come, David found himself standing upon the battlefield at the Valley of Elah before a giant of a man who mocked God and threatened the nation of Israel. David witnessed the leaders of his nation cowardly back down from combat in fear of that monstrous warrior. Confused and tormented by the lack of action from the army that was supposed to stand for the God of all nations, David found himself in a moment that would alter his life forever.

New Normal

Ever have "that day"? The moment when life is transformed into a new normal? Maybe someone you love found out that they have a serious illness. Maybe you lost your job. Maybe you found unexpected distance in relationships that matter to you. Whatever that turning point may be, life delivered you a new normal. Things are comfortable until certain circumstances propel our hearts through the twists and turns of life's rollercoaster.

The news may have first appeared to be good, and then we may have learned that things were not as we thought. What did David think and feel when Samuel anointed him? Was he excited or nervous? What about when he stood toe-to-toe against one of the greatest warriors of his era? Was he overwhelmed with fear?

What about you?

Those days entangle our hearts with heartache, fear, and worry. Unbearable emotions grip the fabric of our being and turn us away from Jesus, transforming our concentration into an agony that continually prepares for the next travesty. Shifting through the ashes of the firestorm that we call life, we are left to ponder the "what if" and "why me" questions.

Some of my favorite memories as a child are the times I played cards with my grandma. Her name was Grace, but she surely did not offer any of it when it came to card games. She always played to win, never playing down to her childish competition. Through those intense matches, I learned a good deal about working through life's difficulties.

We have to play the hand that we are dealt. Life rarely offers mercy and often leaves us wanting to fold because of an unfavorable hand. Sometimes, however, what we have been given is so good that we attempt to coast into victory with little effort.

To win a game of cards, we must play our hand well. We can have the picture perfect hand and still lose. On the flip side, we could have a horrible hand and still win by playing well.

We cannot control what happens in this world or in our lives, but we can control how we deal with those things. We all have a choice. We can allow circumstances to defeat us because we were dealt a terrible hand, or we can play that hand wisely and well. Circumstances do not define us; what matters is how we play our hand.

Life is full of highs and lows. In John 10:10, Jesus says that He has come to give life more abundantly. That abundant life can appear unattainable when the thief rips joy out from under us. Rather than experiencing the abundant life that Jesus promised, we are overwhelmed with shame, bitterness, and the fear rooted in an unwanted past.

My elementary science class did a fun project in which kids would place a stick of celery in a cup of water that is dyed with a particular color. Over time, the piece of celery would transform into the color of the dye as it "drank" the water. The same holds true in our lives. What we invite into our hearts will ultimately become a part of us.

The things that invade our hearts affect how we understand and deal with our circumstances. The future seems bleak when the past is full of undesirable hurdles that left us broken, bruised, and just flat out tired. Experiencing a meaningful life becomes a pipe dream when we fear that each new day delivers some new torture. Our focus turns from Jesus to the struggles we bear.

Joseph's Story

How you deal with those things that lurk in your heart affects how well you can move forward in life. In Genesis, we run into another family that was a bit dysfunctional. The youngest son was named Joseph, and his father had a special connection with him that alienated the other brothers. This created division in the home, and

Joseph's brothers grew to hate him. In the midst of this turmoil, Joseph began to have dreams that put him above the rest of the family, which created more tension. His brothers then made the unimaginable choice to sell him into slavery and fabricate the story of his death.

Evil has a tendency to fester in our hearts. If not controlled, it will boil over into pain and suffering. Joseph's circumstances caused him continual heartache. Life often provides us with undeserved pain. That pain often comes from those closest to us. Our hearts are bruised. It may only take a word, a look, or a flash of memory to bring us right back into our injury.

The pain of our past tends to leave us with shame, bitterness, and fear. As these emotions infiltrate the heart, we attempt to cover it up by seeking approval, pity, or even blaming others.

An unwanted past tends to create pain that, if we are not cautious, can lead to evil in our hearts. Evil growing in our hearts ultimately leads to our own suffering.

Joseph's brothers harbored evil in their hearts. Many were hurt by their decision to sell

Joseph into slavery. Joseph's life was forever altered, and his father's mourning would last for the next 40 years. This ultimately overwhelmed his brothers with grief and guilt.

Uncontrolled evil will terrorize us and deliver us to a shameful pathway. Romans 12:21 states "Do not be overcome by evil, but overcome evil with good." With that in mind, what do you believe is stronger: evil or good? Before you answer that question, investigate your actions. You may say that good is stronger, but how you conduct your life may reveal a different interpretation.

We often live in conflict with Jesus's teachings. In many ways, our lifestyles disagree with our stated beliefs. For example, how do you react when someone wrongs you? Be honest. Is your initial reaction based in love and compassion or revenge?

The way we conduct our lives indicates what may be hiding in our hearts. To defeat the enemy inside us, good must reign. The story of Joseph impresses me. He was a man that was continually put into a place of power. He was sold as a slave to a high-ranking Egyptian official named Potiphar. When jailed, he gained popularity and influence that eventually placed him with Pharaoh as second-in-command over the entire nation of Egypt.

In each of those situations, Joseph was put at a crossroads of choices. At these crossroads, Joseph had the opportunity to do good to others or to finally get them back for the pain they caused him. In every test, Joseph chose to do good and revealed his character.

How different would Joseph's story have been if he gave in and slept with Potiphar's wife? Would he have had a different outcome if he told the baker, whom he was jailed with, a more favorable interpretation of his dream (see Genesis 40)?

Throughout our lives we find ourselves standing at a crossroads of choices. The decisions we make matter. The character of our actions will determine the terrain of our future. We often drive through life on bumpy roads because we toss character aside for what may feel good in the moment. Do you ever take opportunities to ponder your choices? Do you struggle with being completely honest if given the chance to further your gain or to side-step controversy? Do you allow your eyes to wander and pursue lustful ambitions? There are so many seemingly innocent choices that express their counterfeit natures in our character. Think about it, where would those choices lead versus choices pursued with honesty and pure thoughts?

David's Story

We tend to misuse our influence to try to alleviate the pain that festers in our hearts. This never fixes the problem; it only magnifies the hurt. Swallowed up in brokenness, we are left with an opportunity to contemplate the road that led us to this point.

Concealing our pain dominates our efforts as we try to hide lustful pleasures that we sought and dishonest choices that we made. Hiding our struggles' undesirable baggage overwhelms us to the point of complete spiritual exhaustion. David was a man engulfed in distress. Some issues were beyond his control, while others were a direct result of his deeds. While David did wallow in his troubles for a while, he eventually came to the point of brokenness, which led to a lifestyle of repentance.

On the journey to the throne of Israel, David worked through many rough days. At the beginning of his story, a young boy lived with the innocence of a child. As life progressed, the child-like innocence was lost through the complicated reality that we call life. For David, growing up came quickly and harshly.

As a young man, David certainly had hopes and dreams for the future. Never in his wildest dreams, however, did he envision himself sitting on the throne of Israel until Samuel, the prophet, appeared. From that moment on, life would never be the same.

The scrawny shepherd boy quickly grew in popularity after defeating the giant named Goliath. Heralded as a hero, David unknowingly found himself in opposition against the current king of Israel. Saul's jealousy raged, ripping

David's innocence away and leaving him submerged in the reality of hardship and pain.

As we journey through that same world, our lives often succumb to the pain, leaving the mind to reminiscence about the old days, when life was easy and seemingly stress-free. Innocence is often stripped away by one of two factors.

1. When others let us down. David's spirit was let down when he realized the army of Israel backed down from its foe. In similar fashion, we are often left broken when others let us down. It is certain that his brothers and the other soldiers had no idea that their inaction brought David agony. Likewise, those that disappoint us often do so inadvertently and are unaware of their choice's effects.

Despite his disappointment, David took action. The army's lack of action did not restrict David from realizing who was in control of his attitude. Using this moment, David unveiled the foundation of his faith.

What defines your life impacts your attitude. Our daily attitude affects the direction of our faith.

When others wrong us. Unfortunately, we all have a "Saul" in our lives, somebody that is just out to get us. My old high school football coach once told me that in life we will have people that like us and people who don't; many times there is nothing you can do to change their opinions. This is the sad reality of our world. We cannot change what other people do, but we do have full control over our reactions.

Turmoil often generates a course of action, which then enables further torment. Later in life, as king of Israel, David found himself over-looking the kingdom. During a low point in his decision-making, he called for Bathsheba and slept with her (see 2 Samuel 11).

Entangled in controversy, David panicked as he faced his reality. When Bathsheba became pregnant with his child, David called her husband, Uriah, in from battle because David wanted him to sleep with his wife. Being a man of honor, Uriah was unwilling to spend time with his wife while his men were off at war. As David realized his plan had failed, he sent Uriah to the front lines of the fiercest combat, hoping for his death so that he could take Bathsheba in as his own wife. David instructed the commanding officers to pull out of the fight, leaving Uriah completely helpless against the enemy.

David's legacy was thus shadowed by an adultery and murder. That day, that one small mistake could have redefined who he was. Later, when rebuked by the prophet Nathan, David came to understand which reality he had to face.

Broken by the self-inflicted consequences of his choices, David had no one else to blame. Ultimately, he was honest about the mistakes that he made. "For I recognize my rebellion," he said, "it haunts me day and night" (Psalm 51:3).

Honesty is necessary to adequately move forward in faith. Recognizing personal wrongdoings allows us to conduct a realistic evaluation of our current spiritual state. This evaluation is essential to future steps. If we are not real with where we are, it is impossible to correctly identify the next steps to move forward.

We should not, however, allow poor personal choices to hold us captive. We should not live a life of guilt. For any physical body to remain healthy and grow, regular evaluations with the doctor are necessary. Our spiritual well-being is no different. Spiritual check-ups are needed in order for the great physician to guide us towards a spiritually healthy life.

We need to be honest with our sin and hand it over to Jesus. Concealing sin develops unhealthy spiritual habits, which can eventually deter our spiritual growth. Being open and honest about our shortcomings is the first step toward healing.

> "But if we confess our sins to him,
> he is faithful and just to forgive us
> our sins and to cleanse us from all
> wickedness." 1 John 1:9

Through his confrontation with the prophet Nathan, David realized his sin and was honest with God. Seeking God's grace, David began to attempt reconciliation. Making things right is never easy. Pride can interfere and warp our understanding of the magnitude of God's grace. Without Him, we are completely powerless.

Taking steps without His guiding direction will eventually lead to a collapse.

Psalm 51 is a reflection of David's heart at the conclusion of this controversy.

"Have mercy on me, O God, because of your
unfailing love.
Because of your great compassion, blot out
the stain of my sins.
Wash me clean from my guilt.
Purify me from my sin.
For I recognize my rebellion;
it haunts me day and night.
Against you, and you alone, have I sinned;
I have done what is evil in your sight.
You will be proved right in what you say,
and your judgment against me is just.
For I was born a sinner—
yes, from the moment my mother con-
ceived me.
But you desire honesty from the womb,
teaching me wisdom even there.
Purify me from my sins, and I will be clean;
wash me, and I will be whiter than snow.

Oh, give me back my joy again;

you have broken me—now let me rejoice.

Don't keep looking at my sins.

Remove the stain of my guilt.

Create in me a clean heart, O God.

Renew a loyal spirit within me.

Do not banish me from your presence,

and don't take your Holy Spirit from me.

Restore to me the joy of your salvation,

and make me willing to obey you."

Psalm 51:1-12

Making our own rules can misguide us into the thinking that we are the center of attention, yet we are not. Adjusting our situation to match our own terms never works. Sometimes, without realizing, we find ourselves playing God by trying to control the circumstances of our day. As insecurity develops, the urge to control consumes us. Trying to fix our own mistakes often develops more hardships as we try to cover up our sin by committing more sin and causing more personal controversies.

David spent a massive amount of energy and resources in the attempt to cover up his mistakes. We tend to spend so much effort to conceal sins and our shortcomings. In the end, we are often left broken and tired from the never-ending cycle.

The crazy truth is that God already knows what we did and still loves us despite the past. Like David, we need to allow God to create in us a pure heart and renew a loyal spirit, as Psalm 51:10 reminds us.

Life was never intended for isolation. Certain days drop a bomb on us that sends our entire being into a whirlwind of misery. When what you know shatters into a million pieces, let God in to pick them up. That seems so cliché, yet allowing him in can be a major struggle.

God experienced a day when the whirlwind of pain dominated the very fabric of His being. Thunder released a massive storm over the earth as Jesus died on the cross. Overwhelmed with physical and emotional pain, Jesus suffered on that day so that our difficult days do not have to consume us. Can you ponder the power in that?

Take time, like David did in Psalm 51, to reveal your heart to God. Don't allow circumstances to dictate your life. Let Jesus in and allow His mercy and grace to reign.

Personal Reflection

1. What circumstances has life given you?

2. How do you deal with those circumstances?

3. In what ways have people disappointed you? How has that impacted your attitude? How has your attitude affected your faith?

4. Reread Psalm 51:10. Reveal your heart to God.

Chapter 3

THE INJURED HEART

———————•———————

Throughout history, people have attempted to improve the existence of mankind, often at the expense of others. In the efforts to make *our world* better, we found ourselves instilling prejudices on others, thus causing heartache. Through arrogance and pride, discrimination has caused many to stitch together the fragments of their broken lives to seek significance in their existence.

In a survey that I once conducted on the effects of discrimination, there were a couple of comments that stood out as one person said, "For years I had to convince myself that it didn't bother me, that it was no big deal. As the years go on and I learn more about myself I recognize how deeply this has affected me. I felt shame and embarrassment about who I was." Another person even said, "I felt like I had no choice but to be different."

In an effort to take on life, many find themselves repulsed by what they feel is the ugliness of their existence. Abandoned and broken-hearted, too many are left on the search for identity, seeking kindness and acceptance. We may tend to feel, at times, like who we are has been pieced together by fragments of a broken world, only to be tormented with pain and strife.

Like David does in Psalm 22:1-2, we cry out:

"My God, my God, why have
you abandoned me?
Why are you so far away when
I groan for help?
Every day I call to you, my God,
but you do not answer.
Every night I lift my voice, but I find no relief."

Heart injuries can come in all shapes and sizes. From friction in relationships and unmet expectations to the consequences of poor choices, turmoil overwhelms us. Our agony can push us to a sense of abandonment, making it seem like God is a neglectful father falling short on His watch.

Every few years, the world huddles together around its television screens to watch soccer's World Cup. In these long matches, players need endurance to make it through the game and continue on as the momentum shifts back and forth. The teams with greater endurance that respond better to momentum shifts are usually victorious.

We struggle to be content through the momentum shifts of our broken world; we move from good days to days filled with struggles. Days seem to drag on, but years fly by. We cannot sprint this race of life; our endurance will wear out. Life is an extended match that needs emotional and spiritual endurance.

Endurance comes with training. Successful athletes spend countless hours in training to build their physical selves. Without the necessary training, the physical body will wear down, often during the most crucial moments of the competition. Similar training is needed in our spiritual development. Applying God's Word to our lives allows us to maintain our spiritual endurance in those critical moments.

Every day provides a different shift in momentum. Some days go our way, while other days do not. Unexpected, overdue bills arrive, or we suddenly receive bad medical news. If we can deal with the daily momentum shifts, then we can develop a habit of being content in all circumstances.

Amusement parks are fantastic spots for family fun and entertainment. Roller coasters and bumper cars seem do everything right in raising our joy meters. It is almost impossible to jump from ride to ride without being happy. Overloading on rides and cotton candy can take all the world's problems from our minds. When we leave the park, however, reality hits as exhaustion sets in. The children are overly cranky, suddenly feeling what they just spent to enjoy the day. In a flash we can demolish our joy with the new circumstances we face.

Happiness is an attitude that is ultimately affected by our surroundings. "Good days" provide an easier path to happiness. "Bad days" send our perspectives on a detour. To deal with life's momentum shifts, we need to set our frames of reference onto a fixed point. What if, no matter what the day brought, we remained grounded in contentment, knowing who we were and whose we were?

To get extremely basic, if you are not investing quality time in the Bible, then you are missing out on the joy that Jesus gives. We often set our frames of reference on what the media has to say or on what is happing around us. This simply throws our hearts into a revolving door of circumstantial joy. Until we invest in God's Word, not to gain mental knowledge, but rather to adjust our lives according to Scripture, we will not experience real "contentment." We will be tossed around at every momentum shift.

Those that claim to follow Christ often make the excuse that that they just can't find the time each day to read the Bible. Consider the time we spend watching television, going to sporting events, or window-shopping for the latest fashions. Can we find fifteen minutes to read a chapter in the Bible and pray?

The reason we cannot find the time is simply that we tend to treat Jesus like an add-on to our lives. Simply adding Him to an already overly crowded calendar is not the path to success. However, look at how we tend to treat favorite television shows or sporting events. We will cancel things or say no to other events so that we do not miss those activities. Why don't we do the same for Jesus?

If we truly love Jesus, then why aren't we constantly willing to drop something else in our lives to invest in a relationship with Him? Don't we long to spend time with our best friend? Even more so, Jesus longs to spend time with us.

Lifestyle Adjustment

Adjusting our lives to God's standards can be difficult at times because we get in the way.

Think about it, why is it so difficult to express love, peace, and patience? Is it really that hard, or have we become so selfish that we constantly get in the way of God's simplest standards?

For some, it is time to stop debating, stop questioning, and stop being wishy-washy. We know the adjustments that need to be made in our lives. We must stop planning for it and just do it. The time is now.

Our poor responses to this broken world may leave us emotionally off-kilter. We need to alter the course of our lives instead of sinking into the pit of despair.

Saul and David's story demonstrates the destructive pattern of an injured heart. If not tempered, an injured heart will lead to an emotionally explosive fate.

King Saul experiences a subtle shift in character during his story. As he made poor choices, his heart was infested with jealousy, fear, and pride. These feelings develop emotional scars that haunt our thoughts and redirect our steps. Our circumstances can trigger those feelings that create a black cloud over our characters that we may have never even noticed.

Just look at Saul's timeline and how his actions were affected. 1 Samuel 18 reveals a momentum shift in Saul's world. Prior to this chapter, Saul was on top of the world and receiving all the recognition and honor as King of Israel. The young, scrappy shepherd boy named David then entered the scene.

To Saul's credit, he tried to like David, putting on a good front that lasted a while. Over time, however, the emotional scars of his heart were triggered by these new circumstances. An immediate friendship developed between David and Saul's son, Jonathan. David found success in everything he did, causing the people of Israel to sing songs about him, giving him more credit than even King Saul.

The Bible says, "from that time on Saul kept a jealous eye on David" (1 Samuel 18:9). Saul's fuse was lit. Emotional scars festered within his heart, activating less-than-desirable characteristics and determining the person he came to be. These character flaws transformed into Saul's new norm, influencing his decision-making skills. In fact, in the next verse, Saul is described as a madman who raved in his house as he was tormented by the emotional scars that developed within his heart.

Acting like a riptide in the ocean, these emotional scars often go undetected. As the winds of life change, however, the waves of our personal circumstances suddenly pull us further into the deep. Trying to fight the current of this world, we use all our power just to tread water, but it never seems to be enough to recover a state of calmness and contentment.

Overcome

Key steps need to be taken to overcome the emotional scars of our hearts.

Recognize. Acknowledge the existence of emotional scars. These scars originate from all facets of our past, such as a great loss or dysfunctional relationships. If not dealt with, emotional scars have the ability to slowly numb us through constant guilt, anger, and sadness.

Realizing the emotional scars in your heart can begin the process of healing.

Release. Once we identify the scar and its root cause, we need to release it. We must give it over to God and seek help from the church or a good counselor. We often throw our pain at God from a distance. To give us true healing, though, God needs full access into our lives. Allowing Him your heart's full reins is the only way to remove the unwanted junk.

Respond. Despite our shortcomings, God responded to us with love. His love sent Jesus to the cross. How do you reciprocate Jesus's love? Responding to His love is taking the first step to allowing Jesus the full reigns of our hearts. This is a scary process because it involves complete submission to God's standard. God's standard is simple: love God completely and love others as ourselves (see Matthew 22:37-39). To love is to look beyond one's self. Healing begins with love.

To our knowledge, Saul did not make any attempts to heal the scars in his heart. Maybe he just hoped it would all go away, but it never did. Circumstances may never change, but how we respond needs to. The Bible later reveals that David sustained his popularity and Saul became even more afraid of him (1 Samuel 18:14-15).

Reading through this story gives us cause to wonder about Saul, the man. Anyone in a leadership role can attest to how lonely a position it is. At that moment in time, Saul had rejected the prophet Samuel, who was his main advisor. The desire to go his own way was greater than the desire to listen to reason. The Bible does not reveal anyone else with whom Saul had a real relationship. The next possible person was his son, Jonathan, who befriended the very man that triggered Saul's emotional scars. Saul was a man on his own, with nobody to whom he felt he could turn.

Who we surround ourselves with matters. Too often, we push people away because they challenge the triggers of our heart. Maybe we don't like their advice. Maybe they are just getting too close. Maybe we are afraid they will hurt us in the end like so many others have. No matter the reason, we push away the voice of reason and leave ourselves in a state of isolation.

When this happens, our hearts are left to make decisions through a clouded view. The weight of our internal burdens causes choices that set off an emotional explosion, creating collateral damage. Many relationships suffer this collateral damage because people share the burden of their choices with those around them.

Trying to fix his woes, Saul set himself up for destruction. Saul attempted to lure David to marrying into the family with each of his two daughters. He tried to entice David to marry one of his daughters for the mere price of killing one hundred Philistines, soldiers of the great enemy of Israel. Believing that this was an impossible task, Saul envisioned David's demise as he entered the battle.

To Saul's dismay, David not only survived, but also was successful in the task. Becoming even more afraid of David, Saul would remain his enemy for the rest of his life (1 Samuel 18:29).

The bomb exploded in Saul's heart. Reconciliation was no longer possible. The heart's triggers send us into an emotional land mine that sabotages thoughts, choices, and relationships. Falling into an endless cycle of self-pity, resentment, and blame, our hearts become so hardened that they negatively affect all aspects of our lives.

Healthy relationships give way to a sense of isolation as we lose the ability to be content. Joy and contentment are found in a heart that seeks God daily. Yet, because we resent Him for how our lives have turned out and blame Him for our circumstances, we find ourselves pushing God away.

Circumstances in our lives are brought upon by two factors: forces beyond our control and the choices we make.

Sometimes life is unfair. There are forces beyond our control that throw us a curveball. There is no way around this, but we must deal with these situations. In many cases, it is not easy.

While we cannot control what happens around us, we can control how we respond. Moving forward in our lives, we should focus on the things we can control: our attitudes and choices.

Like it or not, we control our attitudes. Whether we got fired at work or someone cut us off while driving home, we ultimately control our reactions to these situational encounters. Look at Paul in the New Testament when he was falsely thrown into prison. He writes, "We can rejoice, too, when we run into problems and trials, for we know that they help us develop endurance" (Romans 5:3).

Contrary to popular belief, Paul did not have a more intimate inroad with Jesus than we do today. He was just a person. What set him apart was an unquenchable passion for Jesus that marked a fixed point on his life's horizon. No matter what happened along his journey, his horizon would not be altered. Because his focus was on Christ, Paul's attitude would not be affected by his circumstances.

Unfortunately, for many of us, we fall into King Saul's trap from the Old Testament. Rather than focusing on Jesus, we adjust our lenses to our daily circumstances. By doing so, we allow for modifications in our attitude that will alter the choices we make. It is absolutely crucial that the lens of our life is fixed on Jesus, not allowing our circumstances to affect our view. With Jesus as our focal point, our circumstances will always give way to the reality that He is in control.

Ultimately, this is part of our spiritual checking account. When it comes to personal finances, we are taught the importance of saving our money. If we develop the habit of saving, then we are prepared to resist something enticing in the mall that would be an ill-advised purchase. Rather than following our impulses, we can save for something valuable than what happens to be in the store window at a given moment.

Our physical eyes are often enticed by the things we see in the world. Life seems unfair when others seem to be getting the better end of the bargain. We choose worldly decisions because we hope to gain those numerous enticements.

Losing sight of our ultimate spiritual reward, we risk the eternal for what feels right in the moment. Saul's story is clear: he lost everything simply because his heart's emotional scars exploded, altering his attitude and adjusting his choices. This settled nothing for him. All it did was add more strife to his life.

At the end of Saul's story was destruction. Investigating your personal path, where are you heading? It is never too late to make the choices that will bring success in your journey.

Do you have a habit of making bad choices? Here's the motto in our family: make the next right choice. Did you mess up? Okay, now what? What do you need to do? Make the next right choice. Repent; apologize. Choose compassion, kindness, and honesty. Make the next right choice.

Personal Reflection

1. With what or whom do you surround yourself? Do these surroundings draw you closer to Jesus or not?

2. What emotional scars are lurking in your heart? Take the key steps to *recognize*, *release*, and *respond* to them.

3. What are you doing for spiritual training? Have you been reading the Bible?

4. How are you allowing God's Word to adjust your lifestyle?

Chapter 4

COLLATERAL DAMAGE

———————◦—————

I ncidental hurt always follows the heart's surge of emotional turmoil. Somewhere along the way, Saul's initial goal to lead God's chosen people changed into protecting what he believed he deserved. David became his intended target.

Collateral damage often occurs in our lives when we lose sight of the actual battle we face. Every day brings an intense battle while we have the breath of life within us. This battle, while not revealed physically, is the fiercest mode of combat this world has ever known. Spiritual forces of good and evil are in a fierce duel for your soul.

As the apostle Paul writes in the New Testament, "For we are not fighting against flesh and blood enemies, but against evil rulers and authorities of the unseen world, against mighty powers in this dark world, and against evil spirits in the heavenly places" (Ephesians 6:12).

This played out in Saul's story when he lost sight of the real battle that he faced. His enemy was not David. His enemy was the evil that infested his heart. As the enemy hid inside, the energy of his efforts shifted from overcoming the evil within to eliminating David.

Realigning his sights on a new target, Saul unknowingly began to hurt other people in his life, from his own children to the people of Israel. Using his daughters for his personal agenda, he attempted to lure David into marriage (1 Samuel 18). He thrust emotional pain onto his son Jonathan by destroying what was a solid friendship (1 Samuel 20). As he focused more on his personal target, he turned his back on the nation of Israel, which he was meant to lead. Even David became collateral damage from Saul's self-conceived mission.

Turning our attention from the actual battle, we unload hurt upon those in our path, leaving a wake of pain that may last a lifetime. Incidental wounds seldom heal from simple gestures of apology. Wounds that cut deep within a person's soul may never fully heal.

Satan is a mastermind of guerrilla warfare. Causing us to shift our attention towards a new enemy, he subtly adjusts our focus away from his existence. We thus waste our emotional and spiritual energy in our confusion over who the true enemy is.

Who Is The Enemy?

Recognizing the enemy is the most important thing anyone can do in a battle. What do we see when we look at the people in our lives that we abhor or with whom we have constant issues? We have more than likely begun to look beyond the person as anything more than a reflection of the things we despise. By doing this, we have blurred our focus. No longer do we see this person as a child of God. We instead see the things we hate, which develops a particular attitude in how we respond. Jesus calls us to pray for our enemies, to love those who persecute us and to do good to those that intend to harm us. By neglecting these commands from Jesus, we have unknowingly hit a pitfall in our spiritual journey. Failing to recognize that good is stronger than evil will send us down an immoral path in the hopes of ending up on top. Ultimately, this belief will determine the trajectory or our lives. Before you jump on the bandwagon with "Sunday School" answers, take a moment to ponder the magnitude of this decision.

Too many of Christ's followers quickly proclaim what should be the correct response: that Jesus is the greatest, that good is greater than evil. Proclaiming these words with their lips, they begin to abandon the most important method of proclamation, which is lifestyle.

What we believe ultimately dictates how we live. If we truly believe that Jesus is Lord of all, then how we live should be driven by what He commands. There is no middle ground. The way we live professes what we believe.

Through the way we live and how we respond to certain situations ultimately reveals whether we believe in Jesus or we doubt that good is better than evil. For example, if I say that good will always win against evil, but then go out and say nasty things about a coworker that offended me, what is my actual belief? Did I not, through my actions, just allow evil to win?

Too often, our lifestyles reflect a different belief than what we proclaim on Sunday mornings. This needs to be adjusted. If we are going to proclaim with our lips that good is better than evil, then we must conduct our lives accordingly the six other days of the week, including what happens when we leave the church parking lot!

Let's return to the question: when we look at the people we abhor, what do we see? For some of us, lens needs adjusting. Each person that we come into contact with, even the one we despise, is a child of God. Jesus died on the cross for that person to give him or her the opportunity of eternal life.

We spend so much of our energy attempting to tear people down, whether to get even or to make ourselves look and feel better. We have blurred our lenses from the ultimate focus. In the Old Testament, Saul totally missed it. He lost sight of his mission and wasted his time and resources on a fruitless chase. We can often do exactly the same.

If we believe that good is greater than evil, then a lifestyle adjustment needs to take place. Rather than getting even or gossiping about those people in our lives, how about we use our time and energy for good? Showing compassion and speaking positively to them and about them should be the trademarks of our efforts. We must focus on the reality that this person is a child of God, someone that Jesus died for. Yes, they may have offended, but what efforts are being taken to lure them closer to Jesus? Have we ever said or done something that may have offended someone? Wouldn't we like them to extend the same amount of grace to us?

Recognizing the enemy matters. It will challenge our daily journeys and it will adjust our hearts. Along with that, it will limit the collateral damage in our lives. Every choice we make affects those around us.

One evening I took my two younger sons with me to pick up our car at the shop. While we were paying, there was another customer that was unhappy with his situation. The environment became tense as this customer burned with anger and began to yell and curse at the shop's employees. My blood pressure began to rise because I wanted to protect my sons from the words that were coming out of the man's mouth. At that moment, I turned and boldly asked this gentleman to be quiet and have some respect for the others in the store.

I then became the focus of his verbal threats. As my irritation grew and the thoughts of what to say next boiled in my brain, I looked down at my two sons. Fear filled their eyes as they waited to see what their dad chose to do next.

Thankfully, their gaze pierced my heart, causing me to simply close my mouth and walk away. The pain that we pass on with our actions is crippling. Actions of good will must win because they send a positive message in a world that constantly expects mischievous actions.

The apostle Paul reveals the importance of preparation for this spiritual battle that we must face. If we take the right steps towards goodness, our actions will turn the potential collateral damage into positive effects.

Look at what Paul writes in Ephesians 6:10-18:

"A final word: Be strong in the Lord and in his mighty power. Put on all of God's armor so that you will be able to stand firm against all strategies of the devil. For we are not fighting against flesh and blood enemies, but against evil rulers and authorities of the unseen world, against mighty powers in this dark world, and against evil spirits in the heavenly places.

Therefore, put on every piece of God's armor so you will be able to resist the enemy in the time of evil. Then after the battle you will still be standing firm. Stand your ground, putting on the belt of truth and the body armor of God's righteousness. For shoes, put on the peace that comes from the Good News so that you will be fully prepared. In addition to all of these, hold up the shield of faith to stop the fiery arrows of the devil. Put on salvation as your helmet, and take the sword of the Spirit, which is the word of God.

Pray in the Spirit at all times and on every occasion. Stay alert and be persistent in your prayers for all believers everywhere."

Understanding the enemy is more than recognizing that Satan exists. We must also realize how he works. As mentioned previously, guerrilla warfare is a tactic in which a small group of combatants use to trick and ambush a larger, less-mobile army. It is impossible to defeat an enemy without knowing their strategies. In similar fashion, we face an enemy whose methods are different than what we generally would grasp. Shifting our understanding from the physical to the spiritual realm, we must understand the devil's tactics.

Satan's Battleground

Satan's main objective is to pull us away from Jesus. His battleground is the mind and heart. The Bible calls the devil the "father of lies" (John 8:44) who "disguises himself as an angel of light" (2 Corinthians 11:14). There are no boundaries to what Satan is willing to do to deceive each of us away from Jesus.

Deception is his weapon of choice. By using things that appear to be good, or that are "not necessarily bad," he encourages our steps to subtly move away from Jesus. They may not be giant steps, but *every* movement away from Jesus is a win for the devil.

Misleading our minds, this master manipulator knows that our thoughts will eventually trouble our hearts and, in time, will redirect our paths. Paul's writing in Ephesians 6 guides us in resisting this enemy. Instructing us to put on the "full armor of God" is not just a fun storyline for a children's class, but an actual call to battle.

Ready or not, the battle is on. The devil is taking the initiative in the attacks on our soul.

Giving us the recipe to resist the enemy, Paul teaches us to stand our ground. Good will win, but only if we are prepared for the battle.

God's Truth should be the foundation of our lives. This world has become extremely diluted with the opinions of others. Everyone has a similar desire to gain the truth that will ultimately bring happiness. Somewhere along the way, truth has changed from a fixed point that directs our lives into an ever-changing viewpoint that gets adjusted with each new desire, leaving humanity in a constant search for peace.

For a person that is lost, which is the wiser choice: to follow one's gut feeling on which way to turn or to get directions from someone that knows the terrain? God is the Creator of everything that exists. He created each individual and the world we live in. Now, who would understand the terrain better, the Creator or one of the creations?

Investing into God's Word is a must if we want to be prepared for this battle. Reading the Bible should dictate the choices we make in our lives. It is written in James 1:22: "But don't just listen to God's word. You must do what it says. Otherwise, you are only fooling yourselves."

Simply having the ability to quote Scripture means nothing if those verses do not change how we live. We must not fool ourselves and just study the Bible. We must invest ourselves in how each passage will adjust the choices we make on a daily basis.

Righteousness

Character and integrity are virtues for which we should always strive. These values are not revealed in how we act when everyone is watching. Integrity and character are developed in the quiet moments of our lives when we think no one is watching.

Revisiting the story of David's encounter with Bathsheba, it appears that David had some extra time on his hands when he was King of Israel and his army was off at war. Sitting on the balcony of his castle, overlooking his kingdom, a young lady bathing caught his eye. Giving in to the temptation, David had his servants bring her to him and he committed adultery with her. She happened to be the wife of one of his closest companions (see the story in 2 Samuel 11).

In that moment of solitude, David lost the battle in his mind and redirected his steps away from God's desire. The guilt of that choice did not just affect David, but also many of the people around him. What must have gone through the minds of the servants who David used to bring Bathsheba to him? As for Bathsheba, a married woman, David was less concerned with her as a person than he was for what he could get from her. Her husband, Uriah, who had given his complete loyalty to King David, was deceived by the king he trusted to cover up the whole affair. We should not forget the nation of Israel, whom David was to lead. Dishonesty and lust are not ideal character traits for a great leader.

In one small moment, when it appeared that no one was watching, David was not prepared. In losing this battle, he created overwhelming collateral damage.

In its most basic understanding, "righteousness" is being right before God. Being right before God builds a foundation in our lives that is the basis of the choices that we make. The choices we make reveal our character and integrity. What we do in our secret place matters. Even when no one is watching, the effects of our actions can be overwhelming.

Right living is an aim that must be guided by God's Truth. We should not equate this with perfection, but rather with the normality of a lifestyle. Generally speaking, does the way we live reflect Jesus's standards or not?

Aiming to live by godly standards steadies our posture, giving us the ability to stand firm when evil attacks. Living by faith is a topic that is talked about in many arenas, but the application of that idea is always a challenge. It seems so easy, yet when the challenges present themselves, we often succumb to fear like the Israelites at the Valley of Elah when they faced Goliath (see 1 Samuel 17).

What separated David from all the trained warriors of Israel on that day? What caused those men that were trained for war to shy away from the battle, while a mere shepherd boy would not be stopped?

Take a step back for a moment. If you were there on that day, where would you be standing? Would you be hiding on the hill with the other soldiers, or would you be running with David to fight?

We often fail to live by faith because our focus has become confused. Everything that Paul reveals in Ephesians 6 as the preparation for battle hinges on Truth, which raises the question: what truth do we trust? Trust is the foundation of faith, as it ultimately reveals whom we follow.

This is the next step after establishing what we believe. We believe in Jesus—that's great—but do we put our faith in Him? This is more than simply trying to treat other people nicely. When the giant comes into our lives, do we trust Jesus enough to follow His lead or do we spiritually stand still, hiding in the distance and hoping the giant will just go away?

There was a difference between David and those other soldiers. Likewise, there is a difference between those that live by faith and those that simply believe, trying to tread water until Jesus comes back. Focusing on God's Truth and investing that wisdom into our journey will push Satan away.

There really is a trust factor. Trusting God is a process in which we all grow. David ultimately trusted God. He believed that God would give him the ability to defeat the giant. He also evidently had faith that was strong enough to go into battle, just as Shadrach, Meshach, and Abednego had enough faith to survive the fiery furnace (see Daniel 3). Knowing their fate, they told the king that they believed that God could save them. Even if he chose not to save them, they would still bow down only to Him.

The faith that people demonstrated in these biblical stories is amazing. Even more amazing is that there was nothing special about David. Shadrach, Meshach, and Abednego were just normal guys. What separated them was the focus of their faith. Even in the most stressful of occasions, their focus was adjusted on their trust in God.

They were able to maintain that trust in the midst of turmoil because they recognized who God was and what He had already done in their lives. When pleading with King Saul to allow him to battle the giant, David recalled God's protection in the face of danger when protecting his flock back home: "The Lord who rescued me from the claws of the lion and the bear will rescue me from this Philistine" (1 Samuel 17:37).

By recalling God's presence in his past, David gained strength for what was ahead. Too often, we lose our faith because we forget how God came through in the past. The Bible says that God is "the same yesterday, today, and forever" (Hebrews 13:8). The way that God revealed himself in the past shows us that He is capable of doing it again. But do we trust Him enough that, even if His direction is different from our desire, we will still walk with Him?

That was the difference between David and the others on the hill; that is the difference between those who journey with Jesus and those, like Saul, who make their own paths when they do not get the answers they want.

In either case, our choices will create collateral damage. If the devil can disconnect our focus from God's truth, then he will eventually manipulate our actions. Taking steps away from God's desire sends a negative message to those in our sphere of influence.

What message does your life send? Will your choices send a message of hope or despair?

Personal Reflection

1. Take a moment to reflect on your life. In what ways have your choices and actions affected others?

2. Do you allow Satan's deceptions to confuse your focus? If so, how?

3. Reread Ephesians 6:10-18. What are three things you can do to stand firm against the strategies of the devil?

Chapter 5

LIVING IN ISOLATION

—————◦:◦—————

D eath. It is a topic that no one desires to discuss, and yet we all must deal with it. Modern technology has helped us better determine the point in which death occurs. Nevertheless, in the most basic of understandings, death is a separation. When the body shuts down and the soul separates, death occurs.

Every person will one day face death. Whether we take our last breath, or Jesus comes back, physical death is inevitable and imminent. There is a second death. The death we do not have to face is the spiritual death. This occurs when our soul separates from God for all eternity. Those who give their lives to Jesus will not experience this.

Many of us, however, deal with an emotional death known as isolation. Isolation is an emotional and spiritual separation that takes place in our minds and our lives. Due to life circumstances, sometimes we experience a spiritual and emotional shutdown. We could be in a busy intersection full of people and feel completely alone.

The Eastern State Penitentiary is located in Philadelphia, Pennsylvania. Opening in 1829, it was the first prison of its kind, moving away from corporal punishment and ill treatment, which was the norm of the day. The Quaker-inspired prison moved beyond the normal practice of punishment in an attempt to create an environment for criminals to spiritually reflect and change their lives. Under a strict policy of isolation, prisoners were never allowed to interact with other people. Complete silence was the rule, as even the guards wore socks over their shoes to dampen any noise when they walked the hallways. The goal was to create an environment of silence and solitude and to expose the criminals to an internal reflection on their behaviors and crimes, causing them to truly be "penitent."[4]

To their dismay, people began to learn that punishment through isolation was not working. In fact, it sometimes backfired, causing the inmates to develop emotional distress and even insanity.

Spiritual isolation hinders our ability to move forward toward Jesus. When our connection with Jesus fails, we tend to transfer our focus from his heart to our own, moving us into spiritual isolation and pushing us to the brink of spiritual death.

Years ago, when the new flat screen televisions were moving onto the scene, I was anxiously anticipating my first purchase. Of course, what would a flat screen television be without updating the cable service? A few weeks into my updated, High Definition cable service, I started experiencing some problems. Certain channels were either slow or just not coming through. Frustrated, I called the cable company to come check my service.

Reviewing my cable connections, the worker hooked up a little machine that read rows of decimals for each line, which represent the amount of power each line receives. Interestingly, there were so many connections that the television line was not getting enough power. Adjusting some of the connections, I was able to enjoy the full magnitude of high definition cable television.

Spiritually we tend to have the same issue. Our lives have become connected to so many things that demand our attention, from work to hobbies and a million other "good things," that we have isolated ourselves from Jesus. Rather than blaming God for what we believe is his inactivity in our lives, we should be checking the power of our connection with him. We are missing out on the fully functioning experience of His Spirit because we are simply juggling too many connections, leaving our faith depleted and unable to stand firm.

Prior to becoming king, David lived a life of isolation under Saul's vengeance. Using all the resources of the nation, Saul made it his life's mission to annihilate David.

David found himself in a state of emotional and spiritual isolation. With the world against him, it appeared that the only people who were on his side were those that emotionally needed him more than they were able to help him.

Being emotionally and spiritually drained is difficult. Others in our lives seem more concerned with what we can do for them than with who we are as individuals. Sitting in the crossfire of an aching heart and the demands of others can send our spiritual lives towards brokenness.

This was the position in which David found himself, hiding in a cave, a man searching for his purpose in life. One moment he was on top of the world, taking on giants, gaining recognition from the nation, sitting at the table with the king. The next moment, he was a fugitive on the run, desperate for food and shelter.

The cave resembles the state of confinement in which we often find ourselves. While in this cave, David wrote Psalm 142, which begins:

"I cry out to the Lord;
I plead for the Lord's mercy.
I pour out my complaints before him
and tell him all my troubles."
Psalm 142:1-2

In this moment, David approached God and began to open up his heart. Many of the Psalms are prayers from David. Through these writings, we get a glimpse into David's heart: his fears, struggles, and triumphs.

Through these prayers, we see an intimacy that David had with God, an intimacy we all long for with the Creator of all good things. His relationship, while not perfect, was real. God was the first person he turned to and the listening ear to his frustrations, fears, and excitements.

Real Relationships

Real relationships evolve around healthy communication. This is the essence of prayer. Prayer is not chanting memorized quotations. It is our means of communicating with the divine

God, who desperately desires a real relationship with us. God is not looking for a repetition of speech; He is looking for people who actively seek His heart the way that He seeks ours. He desires us to open our hearts to Him.

Just examine David's prayer life as revealed in the Psalms. It was anything but pretty. There was a man who was simply laying it all out for God.

Communication is a two-way street that involves speaking and listening. In speaking to God, we have the opportunity to reveal our lives to Him. Yes, God already knows our inner thoughts and the happenings of our lives. He does not seek more knowledge of us as individuals. He already knows it all! Abba, Father, who created us, is interested in developing an eternal relationship with us by sharing His heart with us.

God's ultimate desire is to lead us toward the fullness of life. We can only obtain this by obeying the direction of God the Father, connecting with the sacrifice of Jesus the Son, and following the lead of the Holy Spirit. Knowing

Him more will reveal a love and joy that cannot be experienced through any other manner. Listening to God is rather simple, except for when we overcomplicate it. The main way to hear God's heart is in His Word. The majority of what God wants to reveal to us is unveiled in the Bible. Understanding scripture more clearly will provide insight into the person of God and thus wisdom on our lives' directions.

Developing a healthy prayer life is crucial in our ability to connect with Jesus. It will ultimately keep us from a state of isolation. Here are some steps to develop a healthy prayer life:

Schedule it. Consistency is crucial in any line of communication. Unfortunately, Jesus tends to become an add-on in our lives. Jumbled together with all the other activities on our calendar, time with Jesus gets diluted. To overcome this, schedule your prayer time. Treat it like other priorities on your calendar; do not allow anything else to affect that time.

Throughout the Gospels, Jesus challenged those that desired to follow him to consider their priorities. Jesus demanded that the rich, young

ruler sold everything he owned (Mark 10:17-22).
When others that expressed interest in following
Him desired to reconnect with their families
first, Jesus, in very strong language, expressed
their inability to truly follow Him (Luke 9:57-62;
Luke 14:25-35).

Why was Jesus being so harsh? Simply put,
Jesus demands to be our priority. Challenging
the norms that take precedence in our lives,
like material possessions, comfort, social obli-
gations, family concerns, and sometimes even
"church activities," Jesus yearns to be the top
priority over everything else. Jesus is more concerned about our relationship than our activity.
Activity rarely draws us closer to Jesus; it just
makes us busier. An authentic relationship with
Jesus always moves us towards action instead.
When scheduling activity over Jesus, we often
find ourselves over-stretched, fatigued, and
burdened. There is a reason why Jesus consistently broke from the crowds to focus on His
relationship with God the Father.

In order to fix the mess in our lives and in
this world, we must maintain a real relationship

with Jesus. Until the Creator is involved, we can never expect the routines of life to find harmony. Making Jesus a priority in our schedules and developing that relationship must be the ultimate goal.

Remove all distractions. Those who complete a task most successfully are efficient in removing distractions. From phone usage, to television watching, to the kids jumping on the couch, our lives are overwhelmed with distractions. In the midst of all the noise, we attempt to read our Bible.

For couples who are married with kids, finding alone time on a date night is crucial to the long-term health of the relationship and, ultimately, to the home environment as well. This does not mean that the children are loved less. It means, rather, that in order to be better spouses and parents, we need to take time to remove all distractions and continue to develop a healthy relationship.

Our relationship with Jesus should be treated no differently when, in fact, this relationship is the most important. To maintain healthy relationships with others, we need to strive for a healthy relationship with God. We will achieve this when we spend focused time developing this relationship with as few distractions as possible.

For this to happen, turn off the phone, television, and radio. Distance yourself from things that may fight for your attention and simply focus on God.

Be Real. Oftentimes we build walls with Jesus, keeping the relationship on a superficial level. We may thank him for our food and, from time-to-time, express our requests to Him, but how often do we reveal our hearts to Him? Real relationships express an openness that is not found between mere acquaintances.

We must take caution, because the devil desires to distract us away from a healthy prayer life. Satan knows that poor communication can ultimately lead to a failed relationship. When our communication with God fails, we tend to transfer our focus from his heart to our own, slowly isolating ourselves.

As a teenager, I often ventured out for runs to keep in shape. During one of my jogs, the sun sparkled upon something on the ground that caught my attention. Stopping to take a closer look, I found a handful of quarters. Now this might not seem like much, but to a teenager this was like winning the lottery! Grabbing my newfound riches, I carried on with a big smile on my face. Who knew such a treasure would be right under my feet?

Focus Shift

Even while desperate in the cave, David learned that he was standing on something stronger. Shifting his focus, David fastened his attention to what he had, rather than what he did not have.

The strain of life often diverts our attentions toward worldly problems and away from the God who is in control of all things. At that time, David's life had honestly fallen apart. He had lost everything that he knew and held dear. With an uncertain future, David sat in an unfamiliar and uncomfortable environment. Reflecting on the disarray of his life would have been the easy thing to do.

Sitting in the midst of chaos, David focused on his spiritual journey. Remembering the foundation on which he stood, he redirected his thoughts towards the God who had guided him through every other hardship he had ever faced.

After he acted as if he was insane for fear of the king of Gath (1 Samuel 21:13), David wrote:

"I will praise the Lord at all times.
I will constantly speak his praises.
I will boast only in the Lord;
let all who are helpless take heart.
Come, let us tell of the Lord's greatness;
let us exalt his name together.
I prayed to the Lord, and he answered me.
He freed me from all my fears."
Psalm 34:1-4

When he fled from Saul into the cave, David wrote:

"Have mercy on me, O God, have mercy!
I look to you for protection.
I will hide beneath the shadow of your wings
until the danger passes by.
I cry out to God Most High,
to God who will fulfill his purpose for me."
Psalm 57:1-2
And while in the cave, David wrote:
"I cry out to the Lord;
I plead for the Lord's mercy."
Psalm 142:1

Like David, do you realize that you have the potential to stand on something stronger? In your lowly state, do you chase God?

Unfortunately, we tend to isolate our hearts because we do not truly believe that good is stronger than evil. What we believe ultimately dictates how we live. Our actions test our hearts' beliefs. Claiming an ideology means little if those principles are never applied in our day-to-day lives. Saying we believe in Jesus does not mean a thing if our lifestyles portray a different ideal.

Belief in Jesus is a claim that good is greater than evil. Yet, how we treat others in our lives, from the airport TSA workers to our neighbors who annoy us, relays the true message of our hearts' belief. As our actions exhibit more evil than good, our hearts slowly become isolated, not because God moved further away, but because we did.

Influence Realized

As David chased God, an amazing thing began to happen. Other people joined him in the cave. First his family came to be by his side, and then he was joined by the rejected of the world as "all those who were in distress or in debt or disconnected gathered around him, and he became their commander" (1 Samuel 22:2).

David's first role as commander-and-chief was to lead the so-called rejects of society. Four hundred men joined him. On the run for his life, David was now also called to lead these people. This was not a normal army. These were people with serious problems. They sought something more substantial, and in the cave they found what they were looking for. These people were isolated because of their circumstances, but in the cave they found empathy rather than criticism.

In this cave were the makings of a church. In this moment, God revealed His heart for His people. Church is not about a physical structure. It is the coming together of people with baggage who find strength within God and each other to move forward in their faith.

David was a reject of society who became the leader of the rejected: what a beautiful thing! His misfortunes earned him the credibility to speak for the lives of others going through similar hardships. Others were drawn to this place because they found someone who did not lose faith when the world came crashing down. Here they saw a man whose convictions did not fluctuate with the cultural climate.

Even in a state of isolation, we have influence. Learning to use our circumstances to be a blessing to others is a difficult feat to achieve.

Finding that ability will bring strength in our walk and peace in our hearts.

Through the strength that he had developed, David realized that he could not stay where he was. Stationary faith was a lifeless faith. The time had come to move on and leave the cave.

"One day the prophet Gad told David, 'Leave the stronghold and return to the land of Judah.' So David went to the forest of Hereth."

1 Samuel 22:5

This moment is important. David could have stayed in the cave and hid, but he did not. He did not leave his problems. It was not as though he left the cave and life went back to normal. A new normal would have to be determined. The critical piece to grasp from this experience is that David finally chose to leave the cave.

The cave is reminiscent of the places that we go to hide. It is the place where we ponder our troubles—where we mope—whether it is a physical or emotional place. We often are stuck in our caves.

What defines us is not our circumstances; it is not the past, but rather the foundation that God has instilled within us. David exited the cave to move towards Judah, which by no coincidence means "praise." Throughout this journey, David focused on God and established a strong relationship that would enable him to overcome many obstacles in his path.

God's promises kept David on course. We cannot rationalize God's promises with our circumstances. We must wage war against our circumstances *with* His promises! Working with a young man that he was training to lead the church, Paul wrote: "Timothy, my son, I am giving you this command in keeping with the prophecies once made about you, so that by recalling them you may fight the battle well, holding on to faith and a good conscience, which some have rejected and so have suffered shipwreck with regard to the faith" (1 Timothy 1:18-19).

In the cave, David wrestled with some serious burdens, but he was able to overcome them by chasing God's heart. Moving on from that isolated place, David refocused on God and His promises.

A sense of vulnerability is necessary to move forward in this journey. Victory is not possible without humility. Leaving the cave, David went to Mizpah in Moab and requested that the king allow David's parents a safe haven (1 Samuel 22:3-4).

Easily overlooking the seriousness of this encounter, we tend to miss its significance. David took his parents to a heathen nation for protection, a dirty place with a community of people despised by the nation of Israel. Yet, it was in that place—across the tracks—where David found refuge.

We must lower our pride to seek God. Pride often prevents us from becoming what God wants us to become. It keeps us from building relationships that could be a future blessing in our lives. When pride is stripped away, healing can begin.

To move beyond your cave, it is time to get real with two basic questions:

Do you believe in Jesus? Do you believe that He is the Son of God and that He came to this world and died for your sins?

How has your belief dictated your life? Belief ultimately drives our actions. If you believe something to be true, then it is inevitable that this belief will drive your actions in some way. If you do believe in Jesus, how have you allowed that belief to drive your actions?

Sitting in your cave of isolation, what move will you make?

Personal Reflection

1. Is Jesus the priority of your life or have you allowed activities to consume your focus?

2. Begin the process of making Jesus your top priority. When, on your calendar, can you schedule time to read the Bible and pray? What distractions do you need to remove to focus on Jesus?

3. Are you being real with Jesus? In what ways are you holding back from having an authentic relationship with Him?

4. How can you use your circumstances to be a blessing to others?

Chapter 6

MOVING FROM INFLUENCED TO INFLUENCER

The theme of zombies overtaking society has become a cultural intrigue, one that lays bare the spiritual battle within each of us when that internal struggle transforms who we are as people. Our proximate influences have a tendency to lure us into to being people we never realized existed—people who we hoped we would never become. Zombie-like characters portray an innocence that quickly turns our character into a monster when the immediate environment changes. Likewise, we often find that our moods transform depending on our environment and on the people who surround us.

As mentioned in the opening chapter, we share a similar struggle with the apostle Paul in terms of trying not to fall victim to poor choices by doing the very things we hate. Oftentimes, we succumb to these less than desirable moments because of the influences of those with whom we surround ourselves.

The apostle Paul even mentioned in a different letter, "do not be misled: 'Bad company corrupts good character'" (1 Corinthians 15:33). In many cases, we find ourselves being influenced by those with whom we associate. Jesus, however, calls upon us to be influencers with the message of His love and according to the standard by which our lives should be conducted. Every person is a part of this inevitable cycle. In our lives, there are influencers that direct our mindsets and actions, and at the same time, there are others that we influence. Recognizing our sources of influence affects the way we influence others.

Our lives often reflect the image of our surroundings. Sometimes it appears to be too easy, so much so that the world influences us into a zombie-like state, moving with the noise of human nature rather than the rhythm of God. Living a life of apathy, we find ourselves falling prey to cultural influences that subtly shift our beliefs. When our beliefs shift, the choices we make are altered, which adjusts our paths and ultimately affects future consequences.

Whom we surround ourselves with matters. Filtering the influences in our lives is paramount to our ability to recognize what is right and wrong. In order to move us further away from Jesus, Satan has made our minds his battleground. The devil is a mastermind of brainwashing tactics. Using external means like other people, the media, and music, Satan employs unfiltered influences to send messages and images into our brains. Understanding the complexities of our thinking, the devil simply pushes our thoughts, for he knows our actions will soon follow.

It is a slow process to move from what we once were to the people we claimed we'd never become. It's like the progression of entertainment. Consider the king of rock n' roll. In the 1950's, Elvis Presley made his way onto the Ed Sullivan Show. According to the legend of that appearance, Elvis was only videotaped from the waist up because the movements of his hips were too provocative.[5] In today's television culture, those same gyrations would be a non-issue. In fact, what is currently acceptable has become borderline pornography.

As acceptance grew, the culture was thrust into a downward spiral that transformed what is deemed suitable for television. Working as a master manipulator, the devil aspires to brainwash our reasoning away from God's logic.

As we are easily influenced by our surroundings, it is of the utmost importance that we identify what encompasses our lives. The things that influence us will eventually be the foundation of the influence that we share with others.

Influenced or Influencer?

In every relationship, we are either the one being influenced or the influencer, so we need to ask ourselves whether, in our normal connections with others, we tend to be the influenced or the influencer. There is no middle ground. Each encounter provides an opportunity to make an impact in someone's life, but often all that remains is the reality that our focus is being shaped by the guidance of our cultural surroundings.

While growing in our faith, there comes a time for us to become people that influence others closer to Jesus. The way we conduct our lives is by either moving people closer to Jesus or by moving them further away. Our decisions and our actions affect those around us.

To move from being the influenced to being the influencer, we must first recognize who has an impact on us. Throughout David's story, we see a man who sought the direction of God's influence. A man on the run, David was once again hiding in a cave, where he found himself surrounded by his army and Saul, who had stopped just outside. Because he needed to relieve himself, Saul had entered the cave.

At that moment, danger crept in, danger that evidently challenged David's faith and divided his heart, causing him to be influenced by the men that surrounded him. Sitting in the dark, David's men encouraged him to take action by saying, "This is the day the Lord spoke of when he said to you, 'I will give your enemy into your hands for you to deal with as you wish'" (1 Samuel 24:4).

Conflicted within, David quietly took action by inconspicuously cutting off a corner of Saul's robe. Obviously, David's men influenced him to pursue an ill-advised course of action. However persuaded by their influence, David chose to take that action on his own.

Who Influences Us

Whether we realize it or not, something or someone is influencing us all the time. From our friends, to the media that entertain us, to the magazines or novels that we read, we allow a multitude of influences to wreak havoc on our thoughts. We know we should not gossip, yet we go crazy over media outlets that promote that attitude. Using the excuse that we are just reading the latest news on celebrities, we have taken people created in the image of God and have reduced the status of their existence down to a mere piece of meat, all to satisfy our desire for gossip.

Knowing that we should not commit adultery, we regularly watch television shows that promote promiscuous behavior, and we wonder why we struggle with lust. Though we could continue, I think the point is clear. Making the devil's job easier, we have overwhelmed our minds with unhealthy spiritual influences that have the tendency to push out God's desires. In order to overcome this struggle, realigning our focus should be our main objective.

Broken by his actions, David redirected his focus. After he took a piece of Saul's robe, "David was conscience-stricken for having cut off a corner of his robe" (1 Samuel 24:5). This attitude is crucial to our ability to repent.

In the New Testament, we learn that a major step in giving our lives over to Jesus and following him is repentance. To repent simply means to make an about-face, turning from our old sinful ways towards Jesus. Unfortunately, this has become a practice that many forget to follow. Christianity has been distorted into the understanding that if we quote a simple prayer, then we are good to go with Jesus, yet after we are baptized and after we begin our journey with Jesus, we tend to see little change in our lifestyles. Repentance should completely alter the way we live and speak.

This is what happened to David at that moment. The Bible says that he was conscience-stricken. Like David, we all wrestle with the good angel versus bad angel decisions that we used to see depicted in old cartoons. This is a battle of the heart—of making good choices versus making poor choices. When we weigh out the pros and cons between the two different available paths, we find the battle within.

My teenage years were a classic time that revealed the struggle of living a double-life. Being the good churchgoer, I found myself committing secret acts to gain popularity, of which, deep down, I was ashamed. However, all the while, I attempted to maintain the "good boy" standards with the church crowd. Living a life of dual allegiance, I found myself consumed and defeated.

Attempting to serve both God and man (and self) is a path that many Christians tend to take. While playing the part of a Christian on Sunday mornings, we may often feel/think/act like someone completely different the rest of the week. In allowing this, we must examine ourselves to see if we have pushed our conscience aside, voiding our ability to live a life of repentance and submission.

In reality, because of this lifestyle, we just push God away. To understand our conscience is to recognize that this is the working of God's Holy Spirit. John 14:26 explains the working of God's Spirit in this way, "But the Advocate, the Holy Spirit, whom the Father will send in my name, will teach you all things and will remind you of everything I have said to you."

The Holy Spirit is a fundamental being within the Trinity that we recognize as God the Father, God the Son (Jesus), and God the Holy Spirit. Each part of the Trinity plays a critical role in revealing the glory of God. The Holy Spirit is the "helper" that God sent to guide us toward a lifestyle that honors Him. In times of trouble, God's Spirit protects us; in times of indecision, His Spirit guides us. When we are speechless, He grants us words to say, and when we are lost, the Spirit of God directs our paths.

In the cave, despite the influence of David's surroundings, God's Spirit ultimately convinced David to make the wiser choice, yet in our lives, we have a tendency to allow the influence of our environment to persuade us to veer further from the direction that God has intended us to follow. In so doing, we have muted God's voice in our hearts, leaving us to wander blindly towards our own self-imposed destinies.

When we travel down this road, our hearts harden from the awareness of God's nature as we find ourselves making choices in constant disobedience of His ultimate desire. In the midst of misery, we often question God's existence. As anger brews within our hearts toward the apparent disappearance of God, we may come to the realization that He never actually left but rather that our choices have pushed us away from Him.

After we have learned from David's experience in this cave, we need to reactivate the Spirit's ability to speak into our lives. Listening to our conscience, like David, will lead us back toward choices that can determine once again the direction in which our lives are headed. It was not too late for David to make the right choice in the cave, and it is not too late for you to make the right choice today.

To achieve this, we need to turn down the volume of the world and tune into God. Driving from state to state is frustrating for those who desire to listen to the radio. Constantly going in and out of frequency, drivers are often left with only the noise of static as they strain to catch the final notes of a song.

Our way of life seems to move at 100 miles per hour on a freeway. Running from activity to activity, we find our frequency with God turning into static. Slowing down—adjusting the dial of our souls—can enable us to once again hear what the Holy Spirit is trying to say to us. Every day, He is attempting to communicate. The question is whether we are listening or not.

Listening to Jesus is the beginning of allowing Him to become the primary influence in our lives. Surrounding ourselves with godly influences is the beginning of providing a godly example in the lives of others. The key word here is counsel. It is crucial to concentrate on the counsel of godly examples in our lives. Past experiences and godly mentors provide the wisdom with which our future steps can be guided.

Listening is just the beginning of a lifestyle of faith in action. However, if we do not ourselves make a lifestyle adjustment that points us toward God's desire, then listening is point-less. It is reasoned in James 2:14-25:

"What good is it, my brothers and sisters, if someone claims to have faith but has no deeds? Can such faith save them? Suppose a brother or a sister is without clothes and daily food. If one of you says to them, "Go in peace; keep warm and well fed," but does nothing about their physical needs, what good is it? In the same way, faith by itself, if it is not accompanied by action, is dead.

But someone will say, "You have faith; I have deeds."

Show me your faith without deeds, and I will show you my faith by my deeds. You believe that there is one God. Good! Even the demons believe that—and shudder.

You foolish person, do you want evidence that faith without deeds is useless? Was not our father Abraham considered righteous for what he did when he offered his son Isaac on the altar? You see that his faith and his actions were working together, and his faith was made complete by what he did. And the scripture was fulfilled that says, "Abraham believed God, and it was credited to him as righteousness," and he was called God's friend. You see that a person is considered righteous by what they do and not by faith alone.

In the same way, was not even Rahab the prostitute considered righteous for what she did when she gave lodging to the spies and sent them off in a different direction? As the body without the spirit is dead, so faith without deeds is dead."

Becoming an Influencer

Faith in action is ultimately following God's lead with the choices that we make. In the cave, after being convicted by God's Spirit, David rebuked his men for urging him to take revenge into his own hands. Quickly reading this story today often leads us to be uncertain of the wrestling match within David's heart, causing us to miss the reality of his regret. It's not as if David killed Saul, nor did he hurt him in any physical or emotional way. Simply cutting off a piece of Saul's robe sent David into a tumultuous state of disappointment, and using today's standards, we often overlook the magnitude of this moment, missing the importance of David's renewed plan.

Having realized that Saul was God's chosen king, David knew that it was against God's desire for any person to lay a hand on him. Overwhelmed with remorse, David recognized that his choice separated his heart from God. We cannot take this lesson lightly: cutting off a piece of Saul's robe mattered because God forbid it from happening.

Through our choices today, we often reconcile poor decisions with the mindset that it's really no big deal. We've been left to believe that we can choose our own way to live, thinking that it only affects "my life" and nobody else's. In reality, every choice we make has an impact on our lives as well as those around us.

What influences you and the direction you take each day matter! This is the realization of *your* influence. David realized that the men who influenced him should have been the ones whom he instead was influencing to follow God's lead. The world has the ability to weaken our faith, moving us towards a lifestyle of being influenced rather than influencing. When we move further away from Jesus, those that are following our lead eventually move further away from Him as well.

When we truly follow God's lead, we become an example for others to follow. The problem tends to be that many of us know the good that we are supposed to be doing, but for whatever reason, we are just not doing it.

Somewhere within the history of Christianity, we became warped into thinking that our faith is about how deep our Bible studies are and how much Scripture we can quote. Don't get me wrong: these are all good things, but we read the Bible so that life transformation can happen. As James 2 pointed out, if life transformation does not take place, then our faith is dead!

Following Jesus is not about how much we know. Rather, it is about what we do with the knowledge that we have gained. Giving our lives over to Jesus, we have committed to a way of life that pursues God's mission. His mission is for us to become agents of reconciliation.

After rebuking his men, David "arose and went out of the cave and called after Saul" (1 Samuel 24:8a). This small act revealed a faith that exuded strength in the presence of danger. Walking out of that cave, David was stepping into danger. He was entering a situation that would only be successful if God showed up. That is faith in action because David realized that, once he made himself known to Saul, his life could have been over.

131

Without allowing his fears to rule his actions, David approached Saul to seek reconciliation. As he was moving away from the desire to seek revenge, we see a man who was willing to put his life on the line in order to make reconciliation possible.

God's greatest desire is for reconciliation to occur. This is why He sent Jesus to the world. Jesus reconciles us to God. He left this mission with us: in order to become a person who strives to help others reconcile with God, we need to be able to live in a way of seeking reconciliation with those who have wronged us.

Too often, we live by the worldly standards of being people who fight for "our rights" and "our needs," rather than standing for reconciliation. Creating arguments and disagreements, we have a tendency to build walls rather than develop bridges. The world tends to know more about what we are against than what we are for. Rather than becoming a billboard that advertises what we want changed politically, why don't we try to become agents of reconciliation? Fight to bring God's peace into the lives of people who are hurting, peace that can only be realized through His truth. Then sit back and watch the changes that can occur. We will never see the change in this world that we desire until the King of Kings is the ruler of our hearts.

A crazy thing happened with David's encounter with Saul outside that cave. Rather than finishing his conquest and killing David, Saul "lifted up his voice and wept" (1 Samuel 24:16b). Seeing the heart of God manifested in David's actions, Saul turned from his ways, at least for a moment.

The mark of an agent of reconciliation is a person who chooses to do good even when they are wronged. What good have we done when revenge is the chosen response to an offense? In what way have we helped people know Jesus? Through those actions, we have simply revealed that Christians are no different from the rest of the world, but imagine if, rather than seeking revenge, we made choices to seek reconciliation as David did when he came out of that cave. Just think of the lives that we could change.

Sadly, too often, we become drifters rather than influencers of reconciliation. In the midst of difficult situations with potential conflict on the line, we drift away from the steps that we should take towards the path of what we feel offers the least resistance. When we attempt to avoid conflict, our influence becomes diluted, which creates the potential for more negativity in the future.

In order to move forward as agents of reconciliation, we must first be reconciled with God. The apostle Paul addresses this in 2 Corinthians 5:17-18:

> "Therefore, if anyone is in Christ, the new creation has come: The old has gone, the new is here! All this is from God, who reconciled us to himself through Christ and gave us the ministry of reconciliation."

Consider the actions Jesus took so that we could be reconciled with God. As written in Romans 5:8, "God demonstrates his own love for us in this: While we were still sinners, Christ died for us." This is a drastically different course of action than the trend of human nature. God did not wait for us to say, "I'm sorry." He did not even wait for us to take the first step by making better choices. Though He was the one being wronged, God took the first step towards us in order to make reconciliation possible. In a similar fashion, even though he was the wronged party, David took the first steps toward King Saul to make reconciliation possible. Oftentimes, reconciliation never occurs because we assume no responsibility in the efforts to achieve this goal.

Our Mission

Each follower of Jesus has been mandated with the ministry of reconciliation. We are not called to sit passively on the sidelines, waiting for those in the world to make things right. We are called to step into this broken world to offer a hope that is only found through a relationship with Jesus Christ.

Be warned that this mission requires sacrifice and the willingness to take risks. David risked his life by stepping out of the cave. Jesus sacrificed his life to make reconciliation possible. It is time for Christians to stop attempting to have Jesus while still trying to gain worldly pleasures. Jesus died so that He can have our full devotion. Giving Jesus our full devotion requires a commitment to His mission.

Our ability to influence others is successfully achieved by allowing God to rule in our hearts and to determine our actions. This is not perfection. We see as much throughout David's journey. Remember that, before leaving the cave, David erred and violated God's standard, but what separated David from the others is that he recognized the error of his ways, turned his actions around, and chased after God. He made the next right choice.

All too often, we are too quick to give up when we mess up. Life is not about getting knocked down; it *is* about how we get up. The biggest difference that separated David's path from Saul's was that Saul's poor choices led to more poor choices. When David faltered, he got back up and ran to God.

Do you realize the sphere of influence that you have? Maybe it includes your children, the server at the restaurant that you frequent, or someone with whom you work. Whoever it may be, you need to realize the significant influence that you have in the lives of others. Speaking of your influence, Jesus called you the "salt of the earth" and the "light of the world" (Matthew 5:13-16).

Now is the time for Christians to recognize the significant influence that we have on others. There needs to be an effort to move beyond ineffective influence to an influence that challenges change through a submission to Christ. We often overhear Christians express sadness about the direction of our culture and the world, but until we transform, via submission to Jesus, our hearts and our lives into agents of change, we will not be able to do anything about it.

Now is the time to make a move. Be the influencer that God desires.

Personal Reflection

1. What influences have you allowed into your life?

2. How have the influences in your life affected the way you influence others?

3. Do you have any godly mentors? If not, who is someone that you can ask to be a mentor in your life?

4. What steps do you need to take to become an agent of reconciliation?

Chapter 7

NOW WHAT

———————•———————

C hess is historically one of the world's most popular strategy games. It consists of sixteen pieces, each with individual abilities, with one goal: checkmate. Arguably, the best chess player of all time was Frank Marshall, who reigned supreme in the chess world during the early 1900s. Marshall was best known for his extremely strategic moves, which became famously known as the "Marshall Swindle." [6] A swindle is a deceptive move in which a player in a losing position traps their opponent, thereby turning the game around.

Like the flow in a game of chess, the tides in the game of life have shifted. Living in a chess-like mode, we are in a battle for some-thing far more valuable than a pawn. This spiritual battle is one of intense strategy and spiritual endurance and one that goes beyond the physical realm.

The battle inside is the challenge of looking past the master deceiver who has the ability to take things that appear good and to use them for evil. Fully recognizing his destination, the devil desires to put a move on us so that we may join him for all eternity in suffering.

Trapping us in apathy, he has swindled us into a deceptive comfort. Leading us to think that mere church attendance and good deeds will lead us along the pathway to heaven, Satan has swindled us into the entrapment of hell's gateway. In order to take the next steps in our faith, we need to recognize and guard against some potential traps that have the ability to divert our focus from the One who deserves our attention.

Facing the Pharisees, Jesus attempted to call out particular pitfalls throughout his ministry. The Pharisees were the religious rulers of his day. To the ordinary person, they seemed to possess all the answers and appeared to have an inroad into God, yet they found themselves falling into traps that separated their hearts from God. Their faith was not real. Appearing to be religious was their "god."

One such encounter is in Luke 7:36-50, which recounts when Jesus had dinner at the home of one of the Pharisees. Inviting Jesus over for a meal did not reveal their appreciation for Him—this group definitely was not fond of Jesus. Trying to prove their worth, they often invited special guests over to their house to show off their wealth. They even allowed the poor and common folk to hang out in the court-yards of their homes in order to entertain them-selves as they watched the festivities.

Receiving compliments boosts our self-es-teem and our egos, which we all commonly desire. Like the Pharisees, we at times have a tendency to position ourselves to be certain to receive a boost to our ego from compliments. If we are not careful, attempting to continually be on the receiving end of flattery can become an extremely destructive path as we try to receive love and acceptance. Proverbs 29:5 states, "A man who flatters his neighbor is spreading a net for his steps."

Throughout the Bible, we are introduced to good people who allowed flattery to influence them away from taking the steps that God desired them to take. King Saul was one of those people. The beginning of the end for Saul was when his heart hardened from gaining the flattery that he sought.

Did you catch that at the beginning of this journey? Saul began to lose it when David was gaining the attention that he thought was owed to him. Because of this unquenchable lust for an ego boost, Saul had quickly forgotten whom he was called to serve. We see it with him, saw it with the Pharisees, and tend to see it in ourselves today.

Potential Traps

Flattery is a serious trap that can eventually harm our ability to move forward in our faith.

Along with the desire to be flattered, two other traps can damage our ability to grow spiritually. The second trap involves the assumptions that we create based on what we think we know.

Our sense of reality can be a deceptive trap when we do not secure our beliefs in truth. In the narrative of Jesus dining at the home of a Pharisee, we see this understanding play out.

> "When a certain immoral woman from that city heard he was eating there, she brought a beautiful alabaster jar filled with expensive perfume. Then she knelt behind him at his feet, weeping. Her tears fell on his feet, and she wiped them off with her hair. Then she kept kissing his feet and putting perfume on them.
>
> When the Pharisee who had invited him saw this, he said to himself, "If this man were a prophet, he would know what kind of woman

143

is touching him. She's a sinner!"
Luke 7:37-39

Let's be honest. This woman was a party crasher who created an awkward moment for the dinner guests. Walking into a room of straight-laced Pharisees, this prostitute began to weep, kissing the feet of Jesus and breaking open a beautiful perfume bottle. Could the moment be any more bizarre? Despite the craziness of the moment, Jesus allowed her to proceed with her actions.

Thinking he has Jesus' guilt pinned to the wall, Simon the Pharisee unmasks the self-righteousness of his heart. Never calling this woman by name, Simon simply labels her as "a sinner." The Greek description of this woman emphasizes that she had a notorious reputation around town as a city sinner. Not important enough to be named, the Pharisee simply recognizes her as a street worker. That is all she is known for.

Reducing her to a label, the Pharisee revealed his assumptions based on the reality that he created. His reality was a label, rather than a person. Based on political preferences, religious backgrounds, and lifestyle choices, we fall into the same assumption trap—seeing others for what they appear to be, rather than for what they really are. Dehumanizing others by stripping away their individuality simply reduces them to a stereotype.

Did you see what Jesus saw? He did not see a lifestyle, denomination, or political stance. He saw a person that was broken because they were making choices opposite to God's desires. The world wanted to write her off while Jesus desired to reveal His compassion.

Doing the same thing to David, Saul lost his focus on his intended mission. Rather than seeing the godly potential in David, Saul focused on the potential threat of David's popularity to his own status.

Assumptions can be a dangerous thing. Both Saul and the Pharisees missed some God-sized adventures simply because they had become warped by a self-entertained reality. Largely due to simple differences of opinions, we form assumptions that develop into a reality, which ultimately creates a new doctrinal status that separates us from true reality.

Assumptions are often formed from one of two avenues:

Initial Impression. I am so thankful that my wife did not make her choice based on her initial impression of me. It would have been a done deal. It is a common occurrence and a natural tendency for us to base our beliefs about someone on our first encounter. However, taking the opportunity to move beyond that first reaction provides the ability to open the doors of understanding to new relationships and experiences that have the potential to bring great rewards into our lives.

Throughout our daily interactions, we need to make it our goal to not place labels on others for what they appear to be. Rather, like Jesus, we need to see them for who they are as a child of God who, like us, desperately needs Jesus.

Gossip. Talking about others or providing a listening ear to gossipers is a train wreck waiting to happen. Whether the storylines are true or not, talking about others without a focus on achieving reconciliation is gossip and is extremely dangerous to our spiritual development. Nevertheless, the followers of Jesus continually fall into the trap of forming opinions based on the juicy details that someone else revealed. As Christians, we must learn to control our tongues and must stop providing a listening ear to those who choose to gossip. To listen to gossip is to entertain a sinful choice.

Relationships and good religious organizations have crumbled due to assumptions being made. The problem is that assumptions form a certain belief that ultimately develops a new sense of reality.

Defusing the gossip bomb will strengthen God's Kingdom and provide new opportunities for it to expand.

The final trap to recognize is an unfocused agenda. Claiming to love Jesus, many Christians find themselves sidetracked, completely missing the mission. While dining with Jesus, Simon the Pharisee focused his attention on outclassing this "so-called" Messiah. Knowing Simon's ambitions, Jesus asked him, "Do you see this woman?" (Luke 7:44). Continuing on, Jesus pointed out that this spiritually broken girl from the streets outperformed the self-righteous Pharisee in recognizing the presence of God and in welcoming Him according to the customs of the day. Snubbing the Son of God, Simon's personal agenda distracted him from realizing who was actually dining with him.

In the Old Testament, King Saul was no different. His agenda was seeking glory for himself. Attempting to do just enough to make God happy, Saul evidently believed that he could get away with chasing his desires rather than God.

Saul missed what God had in store for him because envy struck his heart. The Pharisees walked this earth with Jesus, yet missed Him. While living in different eras, Saul and the Pharisees followed a similar path of allowing traps to sway their hearts towards an agenda opposite of God.

Subtle Shift

Sharing in the struggle, we view our aspirations as the center of attention. Finding our thoughts, calendars, and finances controlled by our self-propelled passions, we have methodically pushed Jesus away. Blinded by the self-inflicted traps of our heart, we have completely lost sight of Jesus, even though He is in our midst. As He did with the Pharisees, Jesus is calling us out today, "Woe to you, teachers of the law and Pharisees, you hypocrites! You are like whitewashed tombs, which look beautiful on the outside but on the inside are full of the bones of the dead and everything unclean. In the same way, on the outside you appear to people as righteous but on the inside you are full of hypocrisy and wickedness" (Matthew 23:27-28).

Advancing in the heart, the enemy inside subtly shifts our attention from the mission to the self. This was the primary struggle for the Pharisees and ultimately King Saul. Though he did nothing to deserve the position he received, Saul's passions were entangled in his selfish lust for the attention he received. Since he did not control the struggle, the struggle eventually controlled him.

David, on the other hand, shared similar struggles in his heart. The difference was in his focus. When David messed up, he ran back to God, but Saul never did. There is a significant difference between living a life of repentance and simply being sorry because you were caught. Simply being sorry is only being motivated by the reality of impending consequences. Repentance is an honest sorrow that stems from the actions you committed; it is a desire to never make the same choice that motivates you towards a life change.

King David was not perfect by any stretch, yet he was a man that ultimately lived a life of true repentance. Yes, he suffered some serious consequences that arose from his poor choices, but he never turned his back on God.

When we allow our struggles to consume us within, it ultimately drives us away from experiencing God's mission. Think about it: as Saul focused his attention on killing David, he turned his back on the people of Israel. When the Pharisees spent countless hours trying to debunk Jesus, they continually walked directly past God's intended purpose.

Missing the mission is a serious offense. Self-consumed, we walk past the spiritually broken on a daily basis. As we move further from the mission, we inadvertently cause others to miss the mission.

There are serious consequences when the enemy inside advances. Despite that, the white flag does not need to be raised. The past does not warrant us to giving up. Take a moment to reexamine David's journey:

He was called out of a humble beginning into a great mission for God.

Trusting in God, he stood against many obstacles.

He had the entire arms of a nation fully focused on his demise.

Lonely in a cave, he was surrounded by those that society had rejected. These outcasts eventually challenged God's influence in his life.

Later in life, David was exposed as a liar, an adulterer, and a murderer. Despite those poor choices, this king of many faults was revealed to be a man after God's own heart (see Acts 13:22), a man whom God claimed he was preparing (see 1 Samuel 13:14).

What Do You See

Looking into the reflection of our own lives, we often see a person overwhelmed by the enemy inside. For some of us, this enemy has consumed our hearts, wreaking havoc in our spiritual lives. Overwhelmed by the consequences of our poor choices, we are often left with the question, "Now what?"

What can we learn from David? What separated him from the others? How could a despicable man who committed some grievous acts ever be considered a man after God's own heart?

Again, do not overlook or neglect the importance of repentance. Many of us, like Saul, desire the benefits of what God provides without adjusting our lifestyles. This is just not possible.

Jesus demands an adjustment in lifestyle towards His standards.

This is not about perfection; it is about a humble, grateful obedience. On the Day of Pentecost, standing before thousands of people, Peter gave this call to action, "Repent and be baptized, every one of you, in the name of Jesus Christ for the forgiveness of your sins. And you will receive the gift of the Holy Spirit" (Acts 2:38).

I don't mean to step on any toes, but Christians tend to spend too much time debating grammatical positions, to the point that we have blinded ourselves to action. This verse has generated many debates akin to "which came first, the chicken or the egg?" We have become so consumed by arguing about the timing of the Holy Spirit's arrival that we tend to miss the importance of Peter's call—to repent and be baptized. Does this really require any debate?

I will allow the apostle Paul to convey the importance of repentance and baptism in this journey:

"What shall we say, then? Shall we go on sinning so that grace may increase? By no means! We are those who have died to sin; how can we live in it any longer? Or don't you know that all of us who were baptized into Christ Jesus were baptized into his death? We were therefore buried with him through baptism into death in order that, just as Christ was raised from the dead through the glory of the Father, we too may live a new life.

For if we have been united with him in a death like his, we will certainly also be united with him in a resurrection like his. For we know that our old self was crucified with him so that the body ruled by sin might be done away with, that we should no longer be slaves to sin— because anyone who has died has been set free from sin.

Now if we died with Christ, we believe that we will also live with him. For we know that since Christ was raised from the dead, he cannot die again; death no longer has mastery over him. The death he died, he died to sin once for all; but the life he lives, he lives to God.

In the same way, count yourselves dead to sin but alive to God in Christ Jesus. Therefore do not let sin reign in your mortal body so that you obey its evil desires. Do not offer any part of yourself to sin as an instrument of wickedness, but rather offer yourselves to God as those who have been brought from death to life; and offer every part of yourself to him as an instrument of righteousness. For sin shall no longer be your master, because you are not under the law, but under grace." Romans 6:1-14

Lord of All

Here Paul is revealing the importance of Jesus' lordship in our lives. When baptized, we are revealing that Jesus is our master. Our old selves are gone, and now they are all for Him. Jesus being Lord *of* our lives must develop adjustments *in* our lives. This is repentance.

To the point, repentance is turning away from our old ways and going in God's direction. This is the reflection of David's life. After going in a direction that disappointed God, David ran back towards his King. In his heart of hearts, David's ultimate desire was to please God.

Honesty must spring from within us. In the secret chambers of our hearts, what are our ultimate desires? Repentance will never occur without being fully devoted to Jesus. In all reality, repentance is an issue of the heart. It is the battle within us all.

David struggled and, at times, fell. In the end, he stood strong because he was devoted to God and did not allow the internal struggles to rule his life. Our spiritual journey is not about how we began or even how often we fall. What develops a thriving spiritual development in our lives is a heart that is sold out for Jesus.

Jesus once said, "If you love me, obey my commandments" (John 14:15). Ultimately, what we love drives the way we live. Actions portray the true passion of our hearts. Romantic relationships begin with infatuation—with emotional enticements that leave people longing for each other. This passion ignites a connection, yet like kindling to a fire, it has a tendency to burn out quickly. The work of sustaining relationships needs to be built upon a commitment that can endure when the passion fades.

Many followers of Christ struggle in their journey with Jesus because they construct their faith on emotions. Infatuated by Jesus' all-out efforts on the cross for our sins, we fall into the trap of abusing grace. This occurs when we mistakenly conclude that Jesus' unquestionable love for us means that simply believing in Him guarantees a reservation in Heaven. Jesus was not attempting to build a stadium of believers. His aim was to create followers. This is why, throughout the Gospels, we see several instances of those who are "already saved" losing interest in Jesus. He was simply asking for more than they were willing to give.

Ultimately, abusing grace is a lifestyle built around selfishness. When we assume that Jesus will forgive us because of His love, we move forward with the lifestyle that we desire.

While his eternal gift is free because of His efforts at Calvary, He demands a lifestyle sold out for Him. Realizing the need to carry our cross, we find ourselves overwhelmed by the necessary commitment as our passion quickly fades.

Our Commitment

Later in life, when he was king of Israel, David found himself at odds with God as he, yet again, went against God's wishes. After accepting God's punishment, David was instructed to go to the land owned by Araunah, the Jebusite, and to build an altar upon which to offer sacrifices to the Lord. Upon arriving, Araunah offered to donate his land and the supplies necessary for the sacrifice. However, David insisted on buying it, for he said, "I will not present burnt offerings to the Lord my God that have cost me nothing" (2 Samuel 24:24).

Realizing his commitment, David was unwilling to take the easy way out. Consumerism has the ability to limit our faith from living in full response to Jesus' efforts on the cross. Setting the example for a lifestyle of sacrifice, Jesus calls us to live sacrificially. Giving up our desires to love Him and to love others is the direction in which we are called to go.

Being lured into living for oneself is a victory to the enemy inside. The more that Satan can motivate us to focus on self, rather than on God and others, the more ground he gains in our hearts. Living for the kingdom is measured in terms of obedience. Sadly, obedience leaves a bad taste in our mouths, as the culture shifts more and more away from respect for authority and toward living by our own standards. Venturing down this path moves us further from God and into a reckless future.

However, saying yes to Jesus is making a claim that He is our master. If He is our master, then we are His servants. What He calls us to do, we must do. How He desires us to live, we should strive to do our best. Throughout the Gospels, Jesus reveals that obedience goes with love. If we love Him, then we will obey Him. If obedience to Him is not evident in our journey, then the question of our love should be examined.

This is the center of the battle inside. Think about it: if you truly love Jesus, then wouldn't the normalcy of your life reflect that? Like David, we will fall and will make mistakes. Those shortcomings may invite consequences that we must face, yet in the end, the routine of David's journey revealed a man that loved God above his own desires.

Moving forward in your journey, aim to be a person that continually chases God. Strive to be a person whose day-to-day choices more often than not reflect the heart of God.

In the end, like David, you can stand strong.

Personal Reflection

1. In what ways does your pride get in the way of following Jesus?

2. How have your assumptions shaped your reality?

3. Do you love Jesus? If so, does your life reflect that love?

4. In what ways do you need to become more committed to Jesus and His mission?

Chapter 8

LIVING YOUR STORY

———————◆———————

Each person is a masterpiece on God's canvas of life. Discovering our chapter in God's story reveals the awestruck reality that the Creator of everything that exists has a significant plan for our lives. Unfortunately, like many of our old books collecting dust in the attic, we have hidden away our story for no one to see.

Despite his shortcomings, David strived to live his story. Every good story has a triumph of overcoming the obstacles in the way. Motivation is needed to gain the ability to conquer the challenges that the enemy inside delivers. The apostle Paul encourages those in the Galatian church by saying, "You, my brothers and sisters, were called to be free. But do not use your freedom to indulge the flesh; rather, serve one another humbly in love" (Galatians 5:13).

Coming full circle, motivation is driven by the priorities that define our lives. The Bible reveals that we were called to be free, but what is freedom? Everybody loves the idea of freedom and desires to obtain it in their lives. However, equating freedom with the ability to do whatever we want is a dangerous path. Living "our own way" paves the way to pitfalls of undesirable consequences.

Freedom without boundaries is really no freedom. We live in a world of boundaries, and confusion often sets in when the attempt to achieve freedom lies in an effort to escape those boundaries. Life without boundaries develops traps of our own making. For example, recall when you were a child. At some point, your parents probably had you hold their hands when crossing a street, probably to your dismay.

Even as it provokes fits, parents today continue to do this for the mere desire to protect their children. Parents establish boundaries for their children to protect them from potential danger. While growing up, we never escape the need for boundaries.

Whether or not we realize the dangers, boundaries exist to keep us on the right path, yet like a child, we want our freedom and often come to believe that boundaries restrict us from truly experiencing it. The desire for freedom on our own terms is a slippery slope to disaster.

The crazy truth is that the freedom we think we desire actually restricts us from experiencing true freedom. King Saul learned this the hard way. Thinking he could have the best of both worlds by living on his terms, he in turn lost it all.

In Galatians 5, Paul reveals that living life our way transforms us into slaves. Enslaved to religious practices or to the debts of our choices, the freedom we crave seems to become a distant dream.

Breaking Free

Living for Jesus offers a freedom that breaks us from the yoke of slavery in which we find ourselves. Jesus used the terminology of a yoke to describe those that have become a slave to their poor choices. A yoke was a large beam connecting two oxen to carry a heavy load. Attached to one another, the oxen found no freedom while overwhelmed by the painful and restrictive vice attached to them.

The freedom we try to achieve often restricts us from the freedom for which we actually long. The churchgoers in Galatia struggled as they became enslaved to religious rituals that restricted their relationship with Jesus. They were defined by their religious practices.

In the Old Testament, King Saul was enslaved to his pride, as revealed in his passion for power and popularity. As he lost it all, his failures defined him.

David, on the other hand, failed miserably at times, yet lived within the boundaries that God provided. Despite his shortcomings, he was defined as a man that strived for integrity and character. Recognizing his faults, David always appeared to be a man who strived to make the next right choice.

As you attempt to live your story, what defines you? What is your current state? Are you defined by your political leanings, by how much is in your bank account, or by what sports team you root for?

It is human nature to utilize freedom for indulging our pleasures. When we seek the limelight, our attention slips away from the Provider of freedom and toward the seldom-satisfied desires of our hearts. We can run in circles chasing the latest fads.

It's been said that each of us has a God-sized hole in our hearts. Walking a fine line between living for Jesus and entertaining personal desires, we face a similar frustration to what King Saul confronted when he impatiently waited for the prophet Samuel to come and complete the necessary offerings. It is the unveiling of the true nature of the heart—a desire for personal gain and recognition, rather than pursuing the heart of God. The heart of God is revealed in our love of Him and love of others. When we progress down the path of self-ishness, our faith plateaus as the passion for Jesus fades. The disappearance of passion ulti-mately develops a lack of commitment to Jesus and his mission. This leaves us at the doorstep of a dead faith, inciting Jesus' complaint to dor-mant Christians, "You don't love me or each other as you did at first! Look how far you have fallen! Turn back to me and do the works you did at first. If you don't repent, I will come and remove your lampstand from its place among the churches" (Revelation 2:4-5).

Living for our personal pleasures can cause us to miss out on experiencing our part in God's story. Contrary to popular belief, freedom is not living for oneself. It is an opportunity to be a blessing to others, and blessing others is what serving is all about. Putting others before our-selves is the realization that our so-called rights are insignificant if the cost is other people. Passion for Jesus is revealed in our actions.

To be blunt, King Saul's lifestyle revealed that he was more in love with himself than with God. David revealed the opposite. As you examine your life, ask yourself these questions. What is your passion? With whom are you more in love?

We are God's masterpiece—designed and gifted for a purpose beyond our imagination. Discovering this reality begins with a passion for Jesus. David, like all the other people in the Bible, was an unlikely character that God used to accomplish His magnificent plan. As revealed in the verse from Revelation, Jesus desires to be the primary love of our life, yet like David, we find ourselves consumed with enthusiasm for Jesus while revealing a faith journey full of blunders.

Being a man after God's own heart while committing some serious mistakes reveals there is something more. Through our mistakes, we must find a path towards victory over our blunders.

Leading towards a collapse, pride is often revealed in our attitudes. Thinking they were unsinkable, the crew on the Titanic went full steam ahead into one of the most horrific mistakes in the history of the world. When we struggle with a similar attitude, pride has the ability to blind us to missteps as we try to journey with Jesus. Saul struggled and collapsed. David wrestled with it, but overcame. The difference is with the realization of the struggle.

Proverbs 16:18 reveals that the onslaught of pride paves the way for a life filled with destruction. God is not honored by the proud, but to the humble, he offers grace. Becoming full of ourselves can easily turn us into an enemy of God, as we mistakenly miss the reality of our self-consumed focus, which pulls us away from a true relationship with Jesus.

Pride often leads us to a lifestyle of denying Jesus as Lord. James 2:12 instructs us to "speak and act as those going to be judged by the law." Although many attempt as much, it is impossible to live the double life of following Jesus and living for the world. Countless people try to live this way and unknowingly walk into spiritual danger. As Jesus said, "What good is it for someone to gain the whole world, yet forfeit their soul" (Mark 8:36)?

Moving Beyond Blunders

In realizing our blunders, we can be overwhelmed by a sense of guilt. Saul never arrived at this destination because he was being blinded by selfish desires, thus leaving him with a hardened heart. Guilt is often overlooked when pride reigns within. As if we are splashed in the face with cold water, our guilt awakens the spiritual realization of the mistakes we make, which should move us towards action.

However, do not mistake guilt for the inability to move on from the past. Healthy guilt should motivate us towards better choices, rather than leading us towards the prison of depression. David reveals the pain of guilt as he writes:

"For troubles without number surround me;
my sins have overtaken me, and I cannot see.
They are more than the hairs of my head, and
my heart fails within me.

Be pleased to save me, Lord; come quickly,
Lord, to help me."
Psalm 40:12-13

Sin leads us to grief. God's grace delivers victory. Handing the guilt of our missteps over to Jesus provides a path towards a successful conquest in our spiritual journey.

The persistent nagging of a guilty conscience is a burden from which many Christians suffer. Understanding the value of a clear conscience—and pursuing that ideal—breaks down the wall of spiritual warfare by unveiling the way towards the fullness of life that Jesus promises.

While on trial for his life due to the faith he lived, the apostle Paul shared the efforts of his faith by always striving "to keep [his] conscience clear before God and man" (Acts 24:16). Here was a man, bound for the severe hardships of imprisonment and eventual death, still standing strong, revealing in his testimony the certainty of true spiritual freedom. He showed the ability to break free from the bondage of the enemy inside, realizing that freedom only comes from the capability of achieving a clear conscience before God and other people.

Making a persistent effort for a clear conscience should be our ultimate goal. We see this within David when he was a young boy standing against the giant. Unwilling to settle for the enemy of his nation insulting his God's name, David took action. David knew of God's power and relied upon it to help him strive. Similarly, Christians today should tap into that power by recalling that, as followers of Jesus, we are from God and have overcome the burdens of our own choices, "because the one who is in you is greater than the one who is in the world" (1 John 4:4).

Trusting in God's ability provides the wherewithal for spiritual advancement to take place. Standing still was not an option for David against the giant. It was not even a thought while Paul was on trial, nor should it be an option for followers of Christ today.

Living with a clear conscience is the freedom of not having the weight of poor choices—sin—binding us from becoming the person that God desires us to become. Drawing nearer to God can be a challenge since it involves giving up control of our lives. We know that God is faithful, yet our physical limitations often hamper our ability to realize the vastness of the spiritual capabilities that are beyond our comprehension.

Clay Formation

Isaiah 64:8 provides the understanding that we are merely a lump of clay and that God is the potter, shaping the clay into the formation He deems best. This reality can be a humbling proposition. Let's be honest, God's method of forming us does not always happen the way that we would choose. In those challenging moments, it can be easy to allow our consciences to be defiled, making the poor choices that will one day become regrets. In those moments, David and Paul alike stood strong. We should strive for that strength. Perfection will not always be achieved, but spiritual growth should be evident by making the next right choice.

As followers of Jesus, whether we like it or not, we are being watched. The world is watching to see how real our faith is. Striving to keep our conscience clear before others enables us to set the example.

David found himself in trouble when he silenced his conscience and committed grave sins that affected others around him. Christians' actions and attitudes towards others must be above reproach. Realizing this fact unleashes a livelihood of conveying the truth of God through the examples we set.

Our Reputation

Understanding what it means to be above reproach in our lifestyle may calm some fears. Above reproach does not mean never making mistakes. Instead, it means the normalcy of the reputation that your life delivers. A person may have built a strong reputation of being an honest businessperson, and when someone questions that person's character, possibly suggesting some accusations, those that recognize his or her reputation would not believe the suggestion without undeniable proof.

Sometimes the followers of Jesus fail to realize the importance of reputation. Leaving a poor tip for the server at the diner that we frequent matters in our reputation for Jesus. The words that we choose to use matter in our reputation for Jesus. Thinking through the decisions we make and the impression it may leave on those around us is a significant realization that we need to recognize.

Aligning our lives with the moral code of God is the process by which our conscience is either cleared or defiled. Seeking God's standard of moral absolutes is what Christians should work toward in order to appease a nagging conscience, rather than pursuing today's relativistic call to ignore the pangs of guilt and personal responsibility. It has become a common practice for people who claim to follow Jesus to distort God's standards in order to justify certain lifestyle behaviors, further muddying our relationship with God and our example to others.

Proverbs 16:25 states, "There is a way that appears to be right, but in the end it leads to death." Being blind to our true spiritual state deprives us of achieving the truly authentic relationship that Jesus longs for, and it can potentially lead us towards spiritual death.

The moment of truth has arrived. The chapters have ended on Saul, David, and the apostle Paul, thus turning the pages to our journey today. We have no guarantee of when the story will end, but we have the ability to carry out a positive legacy that will manifest itself in future generations. We have the potential to change the world.

This all begins by not allowing the enemy inside to become your defining feature. Satan does not define your existence. Do not allow him to manipulate the steps you take.

Giving God the control of your life and living life within His boundaries will reveal an abundance of freedom. No longer looking over your shoulder in fear of the past, you can confidently move towards the future.

The enemy inside can be defeated. Let God mold you into a masterpiece, His masterpiece. Then you can realize the story He would like to write through you—a story that will change the world!

Personal Reflection

1. What is your story?

2. What legacy do you want to leave?

3. David turned his mistakes into victories simply by making the next right choice. What is your "next right choice"?

NOTES

1. Disney, Walt, David Hand, Adriana Caselotti, Harry Stockwell, Lucille La Verne, Moroni Olsen, Ted Sears, et al. 2001. Snow White and the Seven Dwarfs. Burbank, Calif: Walt Disney Enterprises
2. Jack Cottrell, The College Press NIV Commentary, Romans Vol. 1, College Press Publishing Co., Joplin, MO, 1996
3. http://www.themoreyouknow.com
4. http://www.easternstate.org
5. http://www.edsullivan.com/artists/elvis-presley/
6. http://en.wikipedia.org/wiki/Frank_Marshall_(chess_player)

ABOUT THE AUTHOR

Bill Balbach is one of the pastors at Impact Christian Church just outside Pittsburgh, Pennsylvania. Through transitioning roles over the years, Bill has had the opportunity to minister to people of all ages and backgrounds.

Bill is a graduate of Cincinnati Christian University and has a Master's Degree from the same university.

One of his smartest life decisions was when he married his wife Shelly. Enjoying a cup of coffee while hanging out with his family is one of his greatest joys.